MW01617922

HARVARD JUDAICA

A History and Description of the Judaica Collection in the Harvard College Library

BY

Charles Berlin

Lee M. Friedman Bibliographer in Judaica
Harvard College Library

HARVARD
COLLEGE
LIBRARY

Cambridge, Massachusetts

2004

Publication has been made possible by
The Sherman H. Starr Judaica Library Publication Fund
in the Harvard College Library,
established by Sherman H. Starr '46.

Dedicated to

All Those
Who Have Assisted in the Development of the
Harvard Judaica Collection

and

Especially to the Memory of

Lucius N. Littauer
Class of 1878

and

Lee M. Friedman
Class of 1893

Table of Contents

Appendices

Preface

Among the strengths of a federal system is the freedom of its components to develop in response to their own internal forces. While significant links to a common trunk bind them together, each branch grows at its own pace. That has been the stimulating element in the evolution of the Harvard College Library and its diverse parts. Those branches are shaped by their exposure to the disciplines they serve, the graduates whose PhDs develop new ideas, and the broader audience, which in Harvard's case is worldwide, for whom the library's collections serve as a repository of past scholarship, often unavailable in their own countries. These collections thereby become also birthplaces for future knowledge and wisdom, expanding information to make it relevant to contemporary issues. The intimate contact with members of the faculty, visiting scholars and a student body drawn from the four corners of the world are the hallmarks of the pluralism, diversity and clash of opinions and ideas which a great university environment facilitates.

Jewish Studies at Harvard is but one department among a multiplicity of disciplines, and the Judaica section of the Harvard College Library is in a building housing millions of books. In common with other collections, though earlier than most, Judaica's holdings have played a significant role in Harvard's intellectual life. Beginning with the college's early days when the Massachusetts Bay was a Puritan colony, the fledgling settlements' scholars and clergy regarded Hebrew as one of humanity's original languages, and their knowledge of Jewish scholarship remained unrivaled for generations. In the intervening 300 years, as Harvard College became one of the world's greatest universities, its library expanded accordingly. And in harmony with the Library's worldwide interests and collections, Judaica positioned its holdings as one of the components in an institution dedicated to an all encompassing vision of human knowledge that covers a multiplicity of languages, faiths and persuasions, and believes in sheltering them all amicably under its hospitable roof.

In a reciprocal response, teachers, students and donors have nourished all of these collections by using them. In so doing, they have deepened their engagement with the past and gained the tools to chart a more secure future. The Judaica Collection is valuable in and of itself, and also because it is part of a worldwide corpus of knowledge, of which the Harvard College Library has always been a foremost custodian and collector. The great institution that the Library is depends on the vitality of its components, of which Judaica is a fine representative.

— OSCAR HANDLIN
Loeb University Professor Emeritus
and former Director of the Harvard University Library
Harvard University

Foreword

The Judaica Division of the Harvard College Library is a truly remarkable division of a truly remarkable library. You hold before you the story of the division and its work. It is written in the characteristically modest style of Charles Berlin, who, like one of Joe Friday's police reports, provides just the facts. It is important that the modest style not distract the reader from the extraordinary story this book tells.

Let me then try to highlight some features of the Judaica Division that make it a world-class operation. The most important relates to collection-development policies and practices. Every university library must seek to obtain as full a collection as it can of the monographs and journals that report the results of scholarly investigation. They advance scholarship, even though they are usually outmoded at some point and become themselves primary source material. Many libraries recognize this, and try to develop as complete a book collection as resources allow. But documenting a culture demands much more than monographs and journals. Visual images of all kinds, music of all kinds, radio and television programs, and, now, websites all are critical elements in the documentation of living cultures. Understanding this, and doing something about it, distinguish the Judaica Division from virtually all other scholarly collections of Judaica (and most other collections of any kind). Nowhere else in the world can one find as variegated a collection of materials relating to Jewish civilization as one can at Harvard.

Secondly, and almost as important, the Judaica Division has collected with great geographical breadth, that is, from all around the world. It has not limited its collection to the interests of current faculty members only; after all, faculty come and go, but world-class collections are designed to last forever. Thus, the Division considers its mandate to collect all that it can regarding Jewish civilization anywhere in the world. That geographical breadth has meant depth of collecting. There has also been depth in the degree to which printed materials have been sought, so that the collection serves scholars in many disciplines. And, as noted above, there has been depth in the types of non-print materials gathered in. In short, the Judaica

Division has documented a culture to a degree that may be unique among American libraries.

Third, the Division has recognized that in order to do its work it must have a strong financial base on which to build; it has worked assiduously to develop that base, as you will read below. This means that the Judaica collecting can go on as long as there is Harvard. The success in fundraising is an important part of the story because it has been so clear to people that the resources have been well spent and accounted for. In other words, the fundraising is part of the story of the creativity and commitment of the Division.

Fourth, the Division has been dogged in its commitment to making its collections accessible as quickly as possible. New Hebrew books get on the shelves with incredible rapidity. Getting books onto the shelves upon receipt has happened not just because the Division's staff are exceptionally diligent but because they are beautifully organized.

Beyond making the collections accessible, the Division has taken on the mandate of providing access to information through public lectures, symposia, and publications, including publications of outstanding undergraduate theses that have relied heavily on the collections.

Finally, all of us interested in libraries know that acquisitions and access are but two of the pillars needed to keep a great collection aloft. Preserving and securing the collection is every bit as vital as acquiring it in the first place. Here again, the Division has distinguished itself, through ambitious programs of off-site storage, through microfilming, and through digitizing.

Accomplishing all this has required a fiercely independent, creative, intelligent, hard-working, and committed approach to collection building and preserving. These adjectives apply to the entire staff of the Division. But great staff ultimately depend on visionary leadership, and that is precisely what the Division's head, Charles Berlin, has provided for more than four decades. It was Berlin who saw the importance of expanding beyond books and into all areas of culture; it was he who refused to structure the collections around transient interests, who knew that a great collection is for the ages; it was he who assembled the extraordinary staff the Division now has; it was he who sold donors on the value of the Division's work; and finally, it is he who keeps the Division fully committed to serving the needs of all users, sometimes exploring far and wide to provide faculty, students, and visiting scholars with what they need. There are indeed not many people of whom it can be said, "All current and future scholars of Judaica are in his debt." But such can truly be said of Charles Berlin, as you will see in the pages that follow.

—JAY M. HARRIS
Harvard College Professor
Harry Austryn Wolfson Professor of Jewish Studies
Director, Center for Jewish Studies
Harvard University

Introduction

When Puritan theologian Cotton Mather (Harvard, Class of 1678) referred in 1702 to Cambridge "being the *Kiriath Sepher* [Hebrew for 'city of books'] appointed for the seat of [the new college]", he did not know just how great a *Kiriath Sepher* Cambridge would later become. He could not have predicted that the Harvard University Library would become the world's largest university library. Neither could he have suspected that the university library in this *Kiriath Sepher* would also be home to one of the world's great collections of the literature of the Jewish people, including a comprehensive collection of books in the Hebrew language, a language greatly esteemed by the Puritans. How Harvard came to have such a collection is the topic of the present volume.

This book has had a long gestation period. For some years now, I have intended to prepare an account of the development of Harvard's Judaica Collection, but the press of work in tending to the Collection's needs always seemed a higher priority than writing about it. Moreover, the fortunate and steady occurrence of new projects meriting inclusion in such an account seemed to argue for postponement. However, the constant urging of colleagues, in the Judaica Division as well as elsewhere, together with the many requests for information about the development of the Judaica Collection, convinced me that this account should now become a priority.

I hope that this modest volume will contribute to the history of the Jewish book at Harvard, with special emphasis on the last three-quarters of a century during which Harvard became a world center for the study of the history and civilization of the Jewish people. This book presents an account of the development of the Judaica Collection, which—as Harvard became a university with different faculties and their own libraries—came to mean the Judaica Collection of the Harvard College Library of the Faculty of Arts and Sciences. Aspects of the Judaica Collection have been treated in various Harvard Judaica library publications such as bibliographic and exhibition catalogs, but there has not been a comprehensive general account. This volume is intended to fill that gap.

In preparing this account, my colleagues and I have become all the more aware of the extraordinary depth and breadth of the Harvard Judaica Collection and of how much more there is to be said about its constituent parts. Indeed, in keeping with a tradition in Jewish literature whereby a text providing a synthesis is an invitation to subsequent commentaries, we hope that this account will encourage more detailed treatment of aspects of the Collection, and that the future growth of the Judaica Collection will warrant a sequel to this account.

I take pleasure in thanking colleagues who assisted in the publication of this volume. Violet Gilboa, Littauer Hebraica Technical and Research Services Librarian, and Elizabeth Vernon, Judaica Technical Services Librarian, both in the Judaica Division of the Harvard College Library, offered constant encouragement, wise counsel, and a critical reading of the text. Elizabeth Vernon also provided the tables and other statistical data, prepared the data for the appendices of events and endowments, assisted in research, and coordinated the copy-editing. Honor Moody, Staff Assistant in the Judaica Division, keyed the text, entered revisions at various stages, and collated the information for the publications appendix. The volume benefited greatly from the editorial skills and expertise of Kenneth E. Carpenter, formerly Editor of the *Harvard Library Bulletin* in the Harvard University Library. I am grateful for all their efforts. For the support, encouragement and inspiration provided by my wife Judy in this endeavor, as in so many others, words cannot adequately express my gratitude.

Of course, the achievements recorded in this volume owe a great deal to the dedicated efforts of the many individuals who over the years were members of the Judaica Division staff, and to the support and cooperation of our colleagues throughout the Library. I would like to acknowledge their important contributions and to thank the current members of the Judaica Division staff—Violet Gilboa, Littauer Hebraica Technical and Research Services Librarian; Judith Kuperwaser, Judaica Cataloger; Mirit Lerner-Naaman, Library Assistant; Honor Moody, Library Assistant; Leah Orent, Hebraica Specialist; Hadassa Schwartz, Hebraica Cataloger; Elizabeth Vernon, Judaica Technical Services Librarian; and our able student assistants. Their daily efforts contribute to strengthening this *Kiriath Sepher.*

— Charles Berlin
Lee M. Friedman Bibliographer in Judaica in the Harvard College Library
Head, Judaica Division, Harvard College Library
Harvard University

HARVARD JUDAICA

Chapter One

Building the Harvard Judaica Collection: Guiding Principles

The Harvard College Library's Judaica Division, since its establishment in 1962, has been guided by various principles that evolved over the years and that were formally articulated in the Judaica Collection's mission statement adopted in 1990 as part of the Harvard College Library's strategic planning process.

Mission Statement of the Harvard Judaica Collection

The Judaica Collection of the Harvard College Library has as its mission the documentation of the Jewish people throughout history in order to support teaching and research at Harvard and to serve as a resource for the scholarly community.

To carry out the mission of the Judaica Collection, the Judaica Division collects in great depth materials covering all aspects of Jewish life and culture in every place and period, with particularly comprehensive coverage of Jewish life and culture in the State of Israel. These materials, from all parts of the world, in all languages, include books, pamphlets, periodicals, newspapers, posters, broadsides, photographs, microforms, sound recordings, videotapes and electronic databases. Special emphasis is placed on materials in Hebrew, particularly from the State of Israel, which constitute the single largest component of the Judaica Collection.

To further its mission, the Judaica Division strives to assure that these materials are available to scholars and students through an efficient and cost-effective collection management program whose chief components are prompt computerized cataloging through HOLLIS (the Harvard Library's online catalog) and appropriate preservation strategies, and through a program of public service that includes bibliographic consultation as well as exhibitions, publications, lectures and conferences related to various aspects of the Judaica Collection.

The Judaica Division seeks to strengthen the financial resources available to carry out the mission of the Judaica Collection through a program that secures Judaica book fund endowments as well as endowments for Judaica library programs and Judaica Division staff positions.

In recognition of Harvard's having a world-class Judaica collection, and especially in view of its having the largest collection of Israeli and Israel-related materials outside of the State of Israel, the Judaica Division seeks to make appropriate and meaningful contributions to the research library community, particularly through sharing Harvard's computerized bibliographic data and through the fostering of cooperative projects with other institutions.

Implicit in the above mission statement is the belief that Harvard should have a Judaica Collection capable of supporting teaching and scholarship in Jewish Studies at the level of excellence expected of all disciplines included within the scope of Harvard's curriculum. Moreover, Jewish Studies, itself a very wide-ranging field, is not an isolated area within the curriculum. Judaism is central to the Western humanistic tradition, and aspects of Jewish history and literature have always been relevant to other disciplines in the humanities and social sciences. For that reason, the Judaica Division has from the beginning broadly defined its collecting scope. It set out to collect Judaica not only in the more traditional areas of Jewish Studies, such as rabbinics, Jewish history, and Jewish literature, but also Judaica in areas such as economics, sociology, and political science. Moreover, the Harvard Library, used by multilingual Americans as well as by scholars and students from around the world, has become ever more international in the languages in which it collects; and that has stimulated the Judaica Division to include Judaica in all languages, in addition to materials in Hebrew and Yiddish. Thus, in language as well as subject scope, the Judaica Collection has broadly supported learning at Harvard.

The Judaica Division has also recognized that the search for "Veritas" ("Truth"—Harvard's motto) requires depth in collecting, because depth affects not only the range of scholarship that can be carried out but also its quality. For the library's users to be able to track down sources mentioned in footnotes or to pursue an idea at the time it occurs is an invaluable boon. To further the range and quality of research by Harvard's faculty and students, as well as by other library users, the Judaica Division has followed a policy of developing a "critical mass," that is, a collection of sufficient scope and depth that research based on its holdings would be sound.

Given its mission—the documentation of the Jewish people throughout history—the Judaica Division recognized the importance of inclusiveness and comprehensiveness in defining Jewish culture for purposes of collection building. The Division has collected to meet the needs of current scholarship, but also—and perhaps more significantly—to anticipate the future needs of scholarship. Indeed, it can be said that the Division has sought to create needs. Tomorrow's scholars might well, independently of library resources, view Jewish culture differently from scholars today, but library resources, in an interactive way, can also shape the questions that scholars ask.

To anticipate needs and to create opportunities, the Division has followed a policy of openness and flexibility with respect to the format of materials collected. In the belief that for most purposes it is content that is important, not the format, the Judaica Division has collected information in whatever format it could be found: printed books, pamphlets, periodicals, posters, broadsides, manuscripts, maps, microforms, photographs, sound recordings (LP, cassette, CD), videorecordings (videotape, VCD, DVD), electronic databases, or Internet files. Researchers do not automatically expect libraries to have materials in all of these formats, but their potential for research becomes self-evident once they are collected.

Printed materials—especially books, pamphlets and periodicals—and manuscripts have traditionally been the mainstay of research libraries, and in the 1960s and early 1970s, the Division's collecting did indeed focus mainly on books, pamphlets, and periodicals in print and microform. The initial emphasis was on trade publications, but gradually the Division expanded into the non-trade material, which functions more as source materials rather than as presentations of the results of research. Recognizing the potential research value of printed Judaica ephemera—ranging from Israeli political posters to Yiddish theatrical playbills—the Division in the mid-1970s broadened its collecting scope to include ephemera, chiefly posters, broadsides, and leaflets. It soon became apparent that a resource for the study of Jewish culture would be deficient if it did not include the wealth of Judaica information being produced in audiovisual formats. Consequently, in the 1980s, the Division added Judaica sound recordings and videotapes to its collecting menu. In Israel and in Diaspora Jewish communities these store and disseminate a broad variety of information, ranging from recordings of Israeli and Jewish popular and religious music and American, European, and Israeli Orthodox Jewish sermons and teachings, to videotapes of documentaries and feature films of Israeli and Jewish content. In the 1990s, it was a natural expansion of scope to include radio and television programs produced in Israel, Europe, and the United States. As new formats have evolved, they have also been included within the Division's collecting scope; most recently the Division has been exploring the possibility of archiving selected Internet websites relevant to the Division's mission.

This emphasis on content also manifested itself in the Division's acquiring vast amounts of surrogate copies of materials. For example, the Division has acquired thousands of reels of microfilm providing access to materials originally found in a wide variety of formats: Jewish newspapers and periodicals in many languages; Hebrew manuscripts; archival collections; rare Hebrew and Yiddish books. Similarly, once information is acquired in one format, the Division may choose to reformat it so that the content may be more accessible or better preserved, as in the case of cassette tapes and old LPs that are digitized to CDs, or posters and broadsides that are digitized. Thus, the Division acquired materials regardless of format in order to assure that the needed content would be available. If the content were only available in a format that was problematic for preservation or access reasons, the Division has addressed that issue with whatever technology was appropriate.

As the scope of Judaica collecting broadened into primary source material, some often produced for fleeting occasions or for a limited audience, the Judaica Division had to adopt a policy of collecting in what has been called "real time." That is, the Division had to establish a network of contacts to monitor what was appearing in various formats and media, so as to gather whatever was issued as soon as it appeared, before it disappeared and became virtually impossible to obtain. A prime example is Israeli election ephemera. The posters, banners, broadsides, leaflets, and other memorabilia intended to assist a party in an election have served their purpose once the election is over; and it then becomes impossible to acquire more than a tiny sampling of these materials. Some political parties disappear if they do not win a seat in the Knesset, and those that are successful by no means invariably maintain an archive or collect comprehensively for it. Judaica Division representatives have to collect this material from each party's office or at the events themselves, if it is to be obtained.

Even current commercially distributed materials require timely acquisition. Many titles are printed in a small number of copies, and publishers frequently cannot afford to maintain large inventories. Delay in acquiring increasingly means that an item will not be acquired. Accordingly, the Division developed a network of vendors who offer materials—current and retrospective—to the Division with an eye to a continuing relationship that would be mutually beneficial over the long-term. The Division has had to sensitize its vendors to the kinds of materials that it wishes to acquire, so that they may take advantage of acquisitions opportunities as they arise.

At the same time, the Judaica Division had to develop another network in order to acquire materials not available through standard commercial channels. This network consists of individuals and organizations that value and are supportive of the Division's mission to document Jewish life around the globe. Included among these materials are the publications and ephemera produced by Israeli and Diaspora Jewish political, social, and cultural organizations, and Israeli governmental bodies. In format, these materials range from reports and pamphlets, to posters, broadsides and brochures, to videos, sound recordings, photographs, and original graphic materials. This has meant effectively communicating the importance of the Judaica Division's mission to a wide range of individuals—government officials, representatives of various non-governmental organizations and associations, media executives, artists, writers, photographers, theatrical and film producers, and librarians and archivists. Many of these people provide materials in their areas to the Judaica Division as gifts or at a nominal cost, because they recognize the value in having their materials as part of the Harvard Judaica Collection to serve scholarship. Their assistance has allowed the Division to build a critical mass of primary materials that it would otherwise have been impossible to acquire.

Similarly, the Judaica Division has long pursued cooperative projects with other Judaica libraries that have resulted in adding materials to the Harvard Judaica Collection that would not be otherwise obtainable by Harvard. Such was the rationale, for example, behind a series of major joint microfilming projects with the Jewish National and University Library (Jerusalem), the Israeli national library, that brought to Harvard copies of an enormous corpus of Israeli press (kibbutz bulletins, local newspapers, historical press). The desire to cooperate also led to joint projects with Gale Tsahal (the Israeli army radio station) and the Jabotinsky Institute (Tel Aviv), which yielded copies of important sound archives. These benefit the scholarly community beyond Harvard as well, particularly because some of the cooperative projects would not have been implemented without Harvard's participation.

Although the Division's mission is to document Jewish life in all periods and places, special emphasis has been on the last hundred or so years. This is a period of unprecedented output of Judaica materials. For example, from an analysis of Harvard's extensive Hebrew holdings, one can reasonably assume that more Hebrew books have been printed since 1970 than in the preceding five hundred years of Hebrew printing. And this does not take into account the enormous quantity of sound recordings, films, videos, and photographs produced in recent decades. Although the "information explosion" of the last few decades in particular has coincided with a period of fiscal constraint in academia, the Judaica Division—with income from its Judaica endowments supporting its comprehensive collecting policy—has been able to acquire more and more materials that are unique in the American and European research library communities. Particular emphasis has been placed on acquiring publications in a wide variety of formats from the State of Israel—the Division's "Documenting Israel" program—and this has resulted in Harvard's having the largest collection of Israeli publications outside of Israel. The Division increasingly finds that it is also acquiring substantial bodies of Israeli materials that are not being collected comprehensively, if at all, by libraries in Israel, such as recordings of popular Israeli music; sound recordings produced in the religious sector; Israeli television and radio programs; posters and other ephemera dealing with politics, culture, and religion in Israel. By focusing on this recent period, Harvard avoids duplicating the efforts of others. Instead, it provides a unique service to scholarship and to posterity by assuring that much material that will be needed in the future for study of this crucial period of Jewish history will be available.

Parallel to the Division's emphasis on building a comprehensive Judaica Collection has been its commitment that everything collected must be accessible for scholars. To meet this goal, the Division utilizes a wide variety of means, from implementation of a goal-oriented, productivity-conscious approach to processing and cataloging materials, to a wide-ranging outreach program of publications, exhibitions, and other events, which bring materials to the attention of the scholarly community.

To carry out its ambitious mission, the Judaica Division early on recognized its obligation to secure the needed financial resources. Although the generosity of an earlier generation provided Harvard with a substantial base, the task of the last forty years—which is, of course, ongoing—has been of such great magnitude that it obviously was essential to secure sufficient financial resources if the goal was to be achieved. Over the past forty-year period, the Division succeeded in obtaining those resources. It created a network of supporters whose generosity in establishing Judaica library endowments and in giving gifts for current use has provided the financial resources that have sustained—and will sustain in perpetuity—the development of the Harvard Judaica Collection.

At the same time, a key factor in the Judaica Division's success has been the way in which it was organized by the Library. The Division has always been a unit in which the staff have responsibility for all aspects of Judaica library operations—including collection development and acquisitions, cataloging, and reference and bibliographic services. To these the Division has over the years added responsibilities in the areas of publishing, fundraising, and outreach programming. Having such responsibility enables the Division's staff to have a total view of the Judaica Collection, which allows

The Staff of the Judaica Division (2004). Left to right: Hadassa Schwartz (Hebraica Cataloger), Violet Gilboa (Littauer Hebraica Technical and Research Services Librarian), Honor Moody (Library Assistant), Leah Orent (Hebraica Specialist), Judith Kuperwaser (Judaica Cataloger), Mirit Lerner-Naaman (Library Assistant), Elizabeth Vernon (Judaica Technical Services Librarian), Charles Berlin (Lee M. Friedman Bibliographer in Judaica and Head of the Judaica Division).

the staff more effectively to build the collection while introducing efficiencies, making better use of staff expertise cross-functionally, and in general being more proactive.

The Judaica Division has always placed great emphasis on the importance of a highly skilled staff as an ingredient essential to the success of the Division's efforts. As the Judaica Collection has grown, and as its Jewish universe has changed—more so in the last half-century than in any previous period of Jewish history—the Division has, happily, found individuals able to cope with the task of assuring the excellence of the Harvard Judaica Collection: people who possess substantial expertise in Hebrew and other languages and have comprehensive training in Jewish Studies and a thorough knowledge of library practices. These staff members have also displayed unlimited imagination, the ability to use technology to good advantage, and the capacity to function with considerable autonomy at a very high level of productivity. "Shared leadership" has been encouraged, and staff are empowered to innovate, to take responsibility for ongoing analysis of workflow, and to make extensive use of student assistants. The Judaica Division's accomplishments over the past four decades are testimony to the commitment of the staff, who have enabled the Division to meet the challenges of the last decades of the twentieth century and who have positioned the Division to meet the challenges of the twenty-first century.

Chapter Two

The History of the Harvard Judaica Collection

The origins of the Library's Judaica Collection may be traced back to Harvard's earliest days. Among the books in John Harvard's bequest in 1638 were a number of Hebrew grammars—a reminder of the great interest of the Puritans in the Old Testament and in its original Hebrew language. Because of the scholarly tradition of Christian Hebraism, the study of Hebrew had been part of the Harvard curriculum from its beginning: from Harvard's first president, Henry Dunster, himself a Hebrew scholar, through the long tenure of Judah Monis, instructor of Hebrew from 1722 to 1760. This tradition was continued by the incumbents of the Hancock Professorship of Hebrew and Other Oriental Languages, a permanent, endowed chair, established in 1764. The study of the Hebrew language was no longer required in the College by 1755, although the minutes of a meeting of the President and Fellows of Harvard College on June 26, 1807 record the following:

> As the Scriptures of the Old Testament were generally written in the Hebrew language – as it is...the original source from which the languages of Europe are derived the knowledge of it is necessary to the divine useful to the scholar & reputable to the gentleman. It is therefore required that the students of the University be instructed in...that simple, ancient & venerable tongue...excepting the Senior Class....But that the President may at the request of their parents or guardians excuse any Sophomores or Junior Sophisters from farther pursuing the study of the Hebrew language....

The College's library naturally included some Hebrew books useful for these Hebrew studies. In 1779, the Harvard Corporation had voted "That the Freshmen be admitted to take out of the Library Hebrew Lexicons, Psalters, or Bibles, for the purpose of Collegiate exercises...." In addition to Hebraica, there were also volumes in other languages dealing with aspects of Jewish history, particularly of the Biblical period, which was relevant to theological studies. The College Library's printed catalog of 1723 listed a number of standard Hebrew rabbinic texts printed in Italy and the Netherlands in the sixteenth and seventeenth centuries, as well as Latin translations of Hebrew texts. Unfortunately, the fire of 1764, which destroyed all of the books in the Library except for those out on loan, destroyed these. A century later, the College Library's catalog (in manuscript) of 1822 listed the following categories of materials in one of the Library's alcoves: "Bibles, Harmonies, Bible Histories, Jewish Histories, Rabbinical Commentaries." It also listed several Hebrew texts printed in Italy, the Netherlands and Germany, while the 1861 report of the Library noted that "alcove 42" includes "Scriptures, Bible dictionaries…Jewish literature, Biblical and Jewish History."

The limited growth that did take place in this early period was shaped by Christian Hebraist studies. Thus, the modest Judaica holdings in the College Library were augmented by the acquisition of Judaica as part of the development of the library of the Divinity School, established in 1826, and by the holdings of the Semitic Department, subsequent to its establishment in 1880. The Divinity School's Judaica holdings were further increased by the merger in 1910 with the Andover Seminary, which created the Andover-Harvard Theological Library. The Semitic Department's collection was rather modest, as Crawford H. Toy, who was Hancock Professor at Harvard from 1880 to 1909, noted in a statement that appeared in the 1879/80 *Annual Reports of the President and Treasurer of Harvard College*: "There is a good working apparatus for ordinary purposes, but much is needed to make the collection sufficient for the ends of scholarly research." The Semitic Department collection was eventually incorporated into the College Library in 1939.

Throughout the nineteenth and early twentieth centuries, a small number of Hebraica and Judaica items continued to be acquired as gifts or as purchases. During the intensive build-up of the Library's East European holdings, which began in the 1890s with the gifts of Professor of History Archibald Cary Coolidge, some 1,300 Yiddish publications were acquired in November 1898. These were the gift of Leo Wiener, instructor in Slavic languages at Harvard and special assistant to Professor Coolidge. Wiener collected these publications in Russia while doing research for his history of Yiddish literature in the nineteenth century. A month later, Morris Loeb (Class of 1883) and James Loeb (Class of 1888), at Leo Wiener's suggestion, gave an additional gift of 700 Yiddish publications. Although several Yiddish linguistic works had been acquired in the course of the nineteenth century, these two gifts mark the beginning of the Library's Yiddish Collection. Thus, by the first decades of the twentieth century, Harvard had the nucleus of a collection of Hebrew and Yiddish books and volumes on Jewish topics in other languages, located chiefly in the College Library and supplemented by the Semitic Department Library and by the Divinity School Library. In later years, small collections of Judaica were developed by other faculty libraries—primarily Law and Medicine—as part of their specialized interest. However, through the first quarter of the twentieth century the Harvard College Library's Judaica Collection for the most part reflected its role as an adjunct to theological studies and to other disciplines.

The year 1925 marked the beginning of a period of substantial growth for the College Library's Judaica Collection. It was in 1925 that Lucius N. Littauer of the Harvard Class of 1878 endowed The Nathan Littauer Professorship of Jewish History and Philosophy in Harvard's Faculty of Arts and Sciences. Littauer was a New York manufacturer, congressman, and philanthropist, whose later gift in 1935 established Harvard's Graduate School of Public Administration. The Littauer Professorship was the first chair in Jewish Studies—as opposed to Semitic Studies—at an American university. Since the Littauer Chair made Jewish Studies a recognized scholarly discipline at the University, it also created the need at Harvard for a collection of Hebraica and Judaica that could sustain research in the many areas of Jewish Studies, not just in those of interest to theologians and Biblical archaeologists.

Over the next quarter century after the Littauer chair was established, the pace of the development of the Judaica Collection intensified. Initially, two small collections were acquired, a gift of four hundred Hebrew books from the library of Morris Z. Alberts, presented by his son, Leon Nathan Alberts (Class of 1909), in 1926, and some 2,600 volumes, including rabbinic texts, particularly oriental imprints, and modern Hebrew literary works, purchased from a bookseller in 1929 by Julius Rosenwald for Harvard in honor of Judge Julian W. Mack (Law School Class of 1887). The opportunity to acquire a much larger collection soon presented itself to the Littauer Chair's first incumbent, Harry Austryn Wolfson. Wolfson had studied in *yeshivot* (rabbinical academies) in his native Lithuania, and in high school in Scranton, Pennsylvania. He attended Harvard University, receiving his A.B. in 1912, and his Ph.D. in 1915. A member of the Semitic Department for many years, he was appointed to the Littauer Chair and went on to become a towering figure in the study of medieval Jewish, Islamic, and Christian philosophy.

Lucius N. Littauer

Harry Austryn Wolfson

The availability of a large Hebraica collection was called to Wolfson's attention late in 1929 by Joshua Bloch, head of the Jewish Division of the New York Public Library. This was the collection of Ephraim Deinard of New Orleans. Deinard was a Hebrew bibliographer, scholar, bibliophile, and bookseller who had acquired Hebrew books on his extensive travels throughout the Jewish world and whose sales of Hebraica had assisted the development of Hebraica collections in many libraries.

After consulting with Lucius Littauer, Wolfson—accompanied by his friend the historian Alexander Marx, librarian of the Jewish Theological Seminary—traveled to New Orleans to see the Deinard Collection. Upon Wolfson's return, Mr. Littauer, acting on Wolfson's recommendation, purchased the Deinard Collection for Harvard. In his letter of gift, dated January 22, 1930, Mr. Littauer noted that he was presenting the collection to Harvard "[w]ith the desire to add to the resources of the Harvard College Library, with a view to creating in the University the possibility of study and research in the various fields of post-Biblical Hebrew literature and thereby increasing the effectiveness of the Nathan Littauer Professorship of Jewish Literature and Philosophy...." Writing to Mr. Littauer on January 30, 1930, Harvard College Librarian Alfred C. Potter acknowledged receipt of "the wonderful gift of Hebrew books that has just been received from you...I feel that the acquisition of these books will prove a great asset to Harvard."

The significance of the Deinard Collection for Harvard was expressed by Professor Robert P. Blake, Director of the Harvard University Library, in a letter of November 23, 1929, encouraging Lucius Littauer to present the collection to the Harvard Library:

> The value of a collection such as this is intrinsically greater when the collection is enshrined in one of the great libraries of this country, such as the Harvard Library is. It is more valuable to those who work at it; the books themselves can be more comprehensively and understandingly utilized in such surroundings; it will give, moreover, scholars in fields other than strictly Jewish studies an unequalled opportunity of obtaining information which would otherwise perhaps be inaccessible to them....
>
> It seems particularly appropriate to me that a collection of this sort should be deposited at Harvard, which was the first centre of Jewish studies in this country, at which have been produced some of the most brilliant and significant studies of Judaism which have been written in America...and where there is now a growing centre of Jewish studies....It will be directly in line, likewise, with the finest trait of Harvard scholarly tradition—a sympathetic and friendly understanding of all the disparate elements which have gone to make up our modern civilization. I can conceive of no way in which a loyal son of Harvard might render a more distinguished service to his Alma Mater than in helping on such a cause.

The Deinard Collection consisted of some 12,000 volumes of Hebraica—most of it quite rare—from all periods and places of Hebrew printing. It also included a few Hebrew manuscripts. As Marx noted in a letter of December 22, 1929, conveying his impressions to Wolfson after their visit to New Orleans:

> The collection is a comprehensive one, including the most important works in practically every branch of Jewish literature....
>
> Deinard...has been able to gather a large number of exceedingly rare and valuable items....
>
> [Y]ou will get a very valuable collection the like of which is not likely to come on the market again.

The Deinard Collection catapulted the Harvard Library into the ranks of the leading collections of Hebraica. It constituted the cornerstone of what was to become one of the world's great Judaica collections, just as the Littauer Chair was the first step in Harvard's becoming a world center for Jewish Studies.

In the 1930s and early 1940s, the College Library continued to acquire Judaica in Hebrew and other languages on a modest scale. Lucius Littauer continued to add to the Hebraica collection. In 1930, he gave to the Library the Fink collection, "nine cases of Hebrew books transported from Germany." In 1937, Mr. Littauer presented the Library with a collection of some 2,300 Hebrew books, including many rare fifteenth- to seventeenth-century imprints, from the library of the late Rabbi Hyman G. Enelow, Mr. Littauer's spiritual guide and friend. Later that year, Mr. Littauer gave the Library three Hebrew incunabula that he purchased from a New York bookseller. Also in 1937, Mr. Littauer provided the Library with its first endowed book fund to support ongoing acquisitions of Hebraica.

The Yiddish holdings also grew, thanks to the efforts of Abraham Aaron Roback over several decades. Roback (Ph.D. 1917) was a psychologist, Yiddish writer, and publisher (Sci-Art Publishers in Cambridge). Author of a history of Yiddish literature, he corresponded with Yiddish writers throughout the world, many of whom sent him their books as gifts for the collection. Roback also sold Yiddish books to the Library through his firm Sci-Art Publishers.

The next major development of Harvard's Judaica library resources came after World War II. From 1949 until 1952, Harvard was the recipient of 1,920 Hebrew books from the Jewish Cultural Reconstruction Organization (JCRO). The JCRO had been established to handle the post-Holocaust disposition of unclaimed European Jewish cultural materials, including books.

Harvard was one of some forty-eight American institutions that were given the opportunity to select books for their collections. In Harvard's case, the books received were chiefly scarce Hebrew books from the various areas of rabbinic literature.

At the same time, the establishment of the State of Israel in 1948 and its emergence as the center of Hebrew publishing created a new source of Hebraica as well as better channels of distribution than had existed previously. The Library, utilizing a combination of direct orders and limited approval plans for Hebrew books and serials printed in Israel, added many current publications to the Hebraica Collection over the next decade or so.

In 1951, the Library acquired the Felix Friedmann Collection, a collection of some 7,000 volumes, chiefly Hebrew rabbinics, but also including many Judaica volumes in other languages and a small number of Hebrew manuscripts. This collection complemented the Deinard Collection, and the two collections together assured Harvard's position as a world-class center of Hebraica. The Hebrew books represented most places of Hebrew printing. The Friedmann Collection was especially strong in Central European imprints—the products of small Hebrew presses in the cities and towns of the Austro-Hungarian Empire—perhaps because many of the books in this collection had been part of a collection assembled earlier by Shelomoh Zalman Ullmann, of Oradea (Romania). The books from Ullmann's collection had been exceedingly well cared for. Many had a distinctive binding, having been bound by a local binder whose label is affixed inside the cover. The Ullmann Collection had become part of the collection of Hebraica assembled by Felix Friedmann in Amsterdam, apparently in the 1920s, which, as was noted in the 1951 *Report of the President of Harvard College,* "was seized and held by the Nazis during the war and brought over from Amsterdam by his family thereafter." A group of donors, organized by an alumnus, Lee M. Friedman (Class of 1893), and at the recommendation of Professor Wolfson, secured the funds needed to acquire the Friedmann Collection from the family of Felix Friedmann.

The year 1957 is one of great significance in the history of the Harvard Judaica Collection. In that year, Harvard was the beneficiary of a bequest by the above-mentioned Lee M. Friedman. Friedman was a prominent Boston attorney, who was an ardent collector of Judaica and had amassed the greatest collection of Western-language Judaica then in private hands in North America. Upon his death in 1957, Harvard received his Judaica collection, which included books, pamphlets, and ephemera in English, French, German, Latin, and other languages printed over five centuries, as well as

Lee M. Friedman

19 January 1949

Mr. Lee M. Friedman
30 State Street
Boston, Massachusetts

Dear Mr. Friedman:

You have asked me to write you in recommendation of the purchase of the library of Hebrew books from the estate of the late Mr. Friedmann of Amsterdam, Holland, for the Hebrew Collection in the Harvard College Library.

By way of a general introduction to the Harvard Hebrew Collection, its history and significance, I can do no better than to enclose herewith a paper on "Hebrew Books in Harvard" which was published in the Harvard Alumni Bulletin for April 29, 1932.

With the acquisition of the Deinard library in 1930, Harvard had come into possession of one of the finest collections of printed Hebrew books. Later acquisitions, especially those from the library of the late Dr. H. G. Enelow, have further enriched the Collection.

The existence of such a valuable Hebrew Collection in one of the world's greatest centres of scholarship and research imposes a sort of obligation upon all friends of Harvard, as well as upon all friends of Hebrew learning, to continue the fostering of the growth and development of that Collection, and never to relax in their effort to enrich its contents by means of new acquisitions whenever the opportunity presents itself.

Such an opportunity presents itself now in the Friedmann library which is offered to us for sale. The acquisition of this library will enable us to start a collection of manuscripts to be added to that of our printed books. The chance is unique. No other assemblage of Hebrew manuscripts of similar size and importance is likely to become available in the near future.

It will also enable us to add to the incunabula and old editions, of which we already possess a considerable number. This is also a rare chance, for soon the market will become depleted of such works.

It will further help us to fill certain gaps in

Letter from Professor Harry A. Wolfson used in the campaign to secure funds to purchase the Felix Friedmann Collection.

the workaday books of our Collection. This is still another rare chance, for most of these books will never be reprinted.

All of these are good and understandable reasons why friends of Harvard are anxious to have these Friedmann books added to its Library.

But to friends of Hebrew literature and learning there are still additional reasons.

The value of Hebrew books, in a certain sense, is intrinsic and does not depend upon the abode of the books. Hebrew books are valuable wherever they happen to be -- in an attic or on the shelves of a private owner, or in the library of a Jewish institution. But their value increases manifold when forming part of a great general library. For Hebrew literature is not the isolated literature of a so-called peculiar people. It is part of the world literature. It has its roots as well as its ramifications in the literatures of the languages of all nations. Hebrew scholars, in their particular Hebrew researches, cannot make full use of their own Hebrew books without resorting to the resources of some great general library; and non-Jewish scholars, in their general researches, similarly often find themselves compelled to resort to Hebrew books. The maximum usefulness of Hebrew books is attained only when placed in a great general library.

Then, also, the safety and security and the proper care of Hebrew books require that they be placed in great general libraries. That was the case in the past. The Jews themselves, in the precariousness of their existence, could not provide their books with proper shelter and security and care. One shudders to think what would have happened to the thousands of Hebrew manuscripts and printed books had they not found shelter in such libraries as the Vatican, the Bodleian, the British Museum, the Bibliothèque Nationale, and many others. Conditions in the world being what they are, such precaution for the safeguarding of Hebrew books in the future is still necessary. These very books offered to us for sale are a case in point. They were guarded for years by Jewish communities or individuals in such countries as Austria and Holland, and still it is by mere chance that just recently they escaped utter destruction.

Sincerely yours,

H. A. Wolfson

medieval and early modern manuscripts of Jewish interest. His bequest also included a special collection on the Dreyfus Affair—the most comprehensive outside of France.

Not only did Lee M. Friedman's bequest make Harvard outstanding in Western-language Judaica, it also provided an endowment sufficiently large to support future Judaica acquisitions, as well as to enable the Harvard College Library to appoint a curator of the Judaica Collection. Friedman's bequest assured for future generations that a librarian would be working to strengthen Harvard's Judaica Collection and would have significant resources to do so.

By the early 1960s, Harvard had thus amassed a substantial Judaica Collection along with several endowments to support the Collection. However, there was no structure yet in place at the Library to further develop Judaica resources in a programmatic fashion. During the 1930s, 1940s and 1950s, the Library had utilized students, both graduate and undergraduate, and from time to time library employees with knowledge of Hebrew, to work with general collection librarians in order to buy and catalog Hebraica. In this way several thousand Hebrew titles were acquired and cataloged. Of course, Judaica in other languages was also added to Harvard's shelves as part of the Library's overall acquisition and cataloging program. Out of awareness that this *ad hoc* arrangement—particularly for Hebraica—was not satisfactory, the Library invited a senior bibliographer at the Jewish National and University Library, Shlomo Shunami, to spend the 1960/61 academic year at Harvard as a consultant. Mr. Shunami focused on technical issues and initiated a conversion of the existing Hebrew title main entry catalog to one in keeping with American standards.

The year 1962 marked the beginning of the programmatic development of the Library's Judaica Collection. Consultation between concerned faculty in the Department of Near Eastern Languages and Literatures and the College Library administration resulted in a decision to establish for the first time a professional librarian's position that would have responsibility for the Judaica Collection. Charles Berlin (Class of 1958, Ph.D. 1963), who had just finished his doctoral dissertation in Jewish Studies in the Department of Near Eastern Languages and Literatures, was appointed in September 1962 as Specialist in Judaica in the College Library. Shortly afterward, the title of the library position was changed to Lee M. Friedman Bibliographer in Judaica, in recognition of the funding for the position provided by the Lee M. Friedman Bequest. At the same time, the Library established a unit, then called the Hebrew Division—headed by the Friedman Bibliographer—

which was to be responsible for the Judaica Collection in general and for the Hebrew Collection in particular.

Initially set up as a division within the Library's Cataloging Department, the Hebrew Division became a separate department in 1974, reporting to the Library administration, as did the Library's Middle Eastern Division and its Slavic Division. This change reflected the multi-faceted responsibilities of these divisions: cataloging, collection development, public services, and a variety of other activities. In 1978, the Hebrew Department was renamed the Judaica Department in recognition of its responsibility for Judaica in the broadest sense, not only for Hebraica. In 1990, as part of a reorganization of the Harvard College Library's administrative structure, the Judaica Department, the Middle Eastern Department, and the Slavic Department were reconstituted as divisions of a new administrative unit—the Area Studies Department, which reported to the Library administration. Berlin was appointed head of the Area Studies Department in addition to continuing as head of the Judaica unit, now named the Judaica Division of the Area Studies Department. This administrative structure remained in effect until May 2003 when reorganization eliminated the Area Studies Department as an administrative unit and its three Divisions—including Judaica—now reported directly to the Library administration.

CHARLES BERLIN

The systematic development of the Judaica Collection that followed the establishment of the Hebrew Division and the appointment of the first Lee M. Friedman Bibliographer is described in the following three chapters.

Chapter Three

The Harvard Judaica Collection: A Description

The Judaica Collection has three major parts: the Hebrew Collection, the Yiddish Collection, and the collection of Judaica in languages other than Hebrew or Yiddish, primarily the so-called "Western-language" Judaica. For the Hebrew and Yiddish books, it is possible to do detailed statistical analyses, since language is coded in the electronic records. The Western-language Judaica materials do not have such a common denominator, and hence statistical analysis of this component is more limited. A description of these three major components is followed by an account of the various special format materials in the Judaica Collection.

The Hebrew Collection

The Hebrew Collection of the Harvard College Library includes over 202,000 titles. There are some 162,000 book and pamphlet titles (paper and microfilm), as well as 9,800 serial titles (paper and microfilm), 22,000 sound recordings (sound discs, cassettes, and CDs), 5,400 videorecordings (videotapes, DVDs and VCDs), 2,300 music scores, 400 CD-ROMs and software, and 170 maps. These figures represent titles only, since the data available from the electronic catalog records do not provide automated counts by volume or piece. Of the 162,000 Hebrew monographs, 155,782 are Widener Library holdings—constituting the seventh largest language collection among Widener monographs. (See Table 1 at the end of this chapter.)

The Hebrew books and pamphlets in the Collection represent all periods and areas of Hebrew printing. However, the number of Hebrew items in the Collection published since 1970 exceeds in number the Collection's Hebrew books published in the preceding five centuries of Hebrew printing. Of the 162,000 Hebrew printed books and pamphlets in the Collection, some 81 percent were printed after 1945, 9 percent in the twentieth century through

1945, 6.6 percent in the nineteenth century, 1.48 percent in the eighteenth century, .4 percent in the seventeenth century, .45 percent in the sixteenth century, and .02 percent in the fifteenth century. (See Table 2 at the end of this chapter.)

The early books, those prior to World War I, were largely published in Central and Eastern Europe, then the largest centers of Hebrew printing, with books from those areas making up 65 percent of the Hebrew books in the Collection published before 1914 (19 percent and 46 percent respectively), although only about 8 percent of the Hebrew collection overall. With the development of the Jewish community in Mandate Palestine and the subsequent establishment of the State of Israel, the latter became the primary center of Hebrew publishing. This is reflected in the Hebraica collection: some 77 percent of Hebrew books in the collection were printed in Palestine/Israel, of which 93 percent were published in Israel since 1948. (See Tables 3 and 4 at the end of this chapter.) Similarly, in the case of the Hebrew audiovisual materials, the largest component is that which is produced in Israel—86 percent and 96 percent respectively of sound recordings and videorecordings. The rest of the Hebrew materials were produced chiefly in the United States and Western Europe, with small holdings from other areas.

The Hebrew Collection covers all areas of Jewish Studies, which may be subsumed under three major rubrics: rabbinic literature (approximately 36 percent of monograph titles held), Hebrew language and literature (approximately 24 percent), and Jewish social sciences (approximately 27 percent). There are also Hebrew works on non-Judaic topics (approximately 10 percent). The subjects of the remaining 3 percent cannot be statistically derived from the reporting program used. (See Table 5 at the end of this chapter.)

Rabbinic literature in the Hebrew Collection is on a wide array of topics. Works dealing with the major texts of the Jewish tradition—the Bible, Mishnah, Talmud, Midrash—account for almost 12 percent of the Hebrew Collection. Jewish religious law—besides Talmudic literature—is the subject of nearly 8 percent of monographs in the Collection (legal codes: 5.7 percent, and responsa: 2.1 percent). The Jewish mystical tradition—cabala and Hasidism—is dealt with in some 3.5 percent. Another 4 percent of the rabbinic literature consists of works in the areas of homiletics and ethics. Finally, liturgical works—prayerbooks of various kinds—account for 5 percent of the Collection. In each category there are primary texts from the earliest to the latest editions, as well as commentaries and scholarly studies.

In the area of Hebrew language and literature, Hebrew literary works account for 14.5 percent of the whole Collection. This category includes poetry, fiction and drama from all periods, as well as literary studies, with modern Hebrew (including Israeli) literary works the largest component. Hebrew children's literature, which comprises nearly 8 percent of the Hebrew Collection consists of original Hebrew works, chiefly Israeli, for all age levels, as well as translations into Hebrew of children's books published in other languages. Reference works and studies on the Hebrew language, some 2 percent of the Hebrew Collection, include Hebrew grammars, dictionaries—especially of Hebrew into other languages, and of other languages into Hebrew—and studies of various aspects of the Hebrew language.

In this description of the Hebrew Collection, the term "Jewish social sciences" is used to refer to works dealing with Jewish history, politics, sociology, economics, and the arts, i.e., all aspects of Jewish civilization except rabbinic literature and Hebrew language and literature. Over 5 percent of the Hebrew Collection (20 percent of the Jewish social science materials) is made up of works dealing with the various aspects of Jewish civilization in the Diaspora. Over 93 percent of the Jewish social science materials deals with Jewish life in Israel. The latter—some 20 percent of the Hebrew Collection—consists of publications dealing with all aspects of the State of Israel—economy; sociology; the arts; education; biography; and histories of the State of Israel and its various cities, towns and kibbutzim. There is a wide range of types of materials: scholarly studies, popular works, publications of government ministries and municipalities, prospectuses and financial reports of corporations, kibbutz memorial volumes, art gallery and museum catalogs, school textbooks, publications of organizations and associations, and cookbooks.

Some 10 percent of the Hebrew Collection consists of Hebrew books on non-Judaic themes. These are primarily Hebrew translations of works in the humanities, social sciences, and science that have no relationship to Judaica or Jewish Studies but have been translated into Hebrew as part of Jewish interaction with other cultures. Although there are translations from every period of Jewish history, the largest portion by far consists of Hebrew translations published in Israel. These translations document cultural transmission as well as the development of the Hebrew language. In addition to the translations, there are also many original works in Hebrew on non-Judaic topics, both scholarly monographs and popular works.

In addition to books and pamphlets, the Hebrew Collection includes some 9,800 Hebrew serial titles (including microform copies) published throughout the world. These consist of newspapers and periodicals and include dailies, weeklies, monthlies, annuals, among others. These diverse serials include scholarly journals in various areas of Jewish Studies such as rabbinics, Hebrew literature and Jewish history; Hebrew newspapers from nineteenth-century Eastern Europe to contemporary Israel; Israeli literary, political and economic journals, popular magazines, and organizational bulletins.

The Yiddish Collection

The Yiddish Collection consists of some 22,000 books and pamphlets, 3,600 serials, 5,000 sound recordings, 130 videorecordings, and 1,600 music scores. Most of the Yiddish printed materials were published before 1945 (62 percent), with over 95 percent published before 1985. Most are Yiddish literary works—novels, stories, poetry, and drama. Some 40 percent were printed in Eastern Europe, 30 percent in the United States, 10 percent in Israel, 8 percent in Latin America, and the remainder in Western Europe, Central Europe, Canada, Australia, South Africa, and the Far East.

Judaica in Other Languages

As noted above, the Library's online catalog reporting mechanism does not provide for a comprehensive statistical retrieval of Judaica in languages other than Hebrew and Yiddish, but it is estimated that there are some 200,000 titles. Large collections are held in English, French, German, Russian, and Spanish; smaller ones in Arabic, Danish, Dutch, Hungarian, Italian, Latin, Polish, Portuguese, Romanian, Ukrainian, and other languages. In addition, the collection includes some 1,300 Hebrew-script titles in languages other than Hebrew and Yiddish: Ladino (1,010), Judeo-Arabic (252), and Judeo-Persian (29).

These materials, covering the entire five and a half centuries of printing, were published all over the world, and deal with all aspects of Jewish history and culture. Understandably, many of these publications focus on the local Jewish communities. Thus, Spanish materials from Argentina include many publications of the Argentine Jewish organizations in Buenos Aires and other cities, such as reports of the central community organization, pamphlets issued by Jewish educational and religious institutions, and by-laws of various Jewish social and charitable groups. Similar materials are found in virtually all the languages. Numerous local histories exist in each language. There are also literary works on Jewish themes. There are many translations of Judaica originally published in other languages, especially Hebrew and

Yiddish—documentation of the effort to overcome language barriers in the transmission of Jewish culture from one Jewish community to another. Each language includes many original works of scholarship dealing with Jewish philosophy, theology, history, and rabbinics—all contributions of each language community to the corpus of Jewish culture. Especially noteworthy in the collection are materials in languages that are not readily available in most Judaica collections, such as Danish, Dutch, Hungarian, and Romanian. Besides books and pamphlets, there are large collections of serials, microforms, and audiovisual materials, plus ephemera, in the various languages comprising the Judaica component of the collection.

Special Formats

The Judaica Collection has been enhanced by the Division's efforts to acquire materials besides books, pamphlets, and periodicals. These materials include microforms, sound recordings, videotapes, CD-ROMs, ephemera (posters, broadsides, etc.), photographs, manuscripts, artwork, and Jewish ceremonial objects. Judaica materials in these formats have added much to the Judaica Collection's capacity to support research, particularly in the modern period.

Microforms

In addition to its role as a preservation tool, which will be discussed later, microform has been essential to building the Judaica Collection: it has made it possible to acquire copies of materials that could not be acquired in the original. These have amounted to thousands of reels of microfilm and sheets of microfiche. The Harvard Judaica Collection includes some 11,000 Hebrew monograph microfilm titles (5,000 held only in microfilm; 6,100 in both microfilm and paper), 8,800 Yiddish monograph microfilm titles (5,500 held only in microfilm; 3,300 in microfilm and paper), 1,200 Hebrew serial microfilm titles (500 held only in microfilm; 700 held at least in part in both paper and microfilm), and 2,400 Yiddish serial microfilm titles (1,900 held only in microfilm; 500 held at least in part in both paper and microfilm). Although the above type of statistics is not readily available for non-Hebraica microfilm holdings, holdings of the latter are also very extensive.

Microforms have been especially important in the case of newspapers. The Division has been able to build a vast collection of the Jewish press in microfilm: Hebrew newspapers from the early Jewish community in the Land of Israel and later the State of Israel; Yiddish newspapers from Eastern

Europe, North and South America, and elsewhere; European Jewish newspapers in Dutch, English, French, German, Polish, Romanian, Russian, and other languages; the American Jewish press; and Ladino and Judeo-Arabic newspapers. Similarly, microfilm has made possible the acquisition of thousands of Jewish periodicals and magazines in Hebrew, Yiddish, and other languages. This is also the case with regard to the many Israeli local newspapers and the bulletins of the various kibbutzim in Israel—both acquired through a joint microfilming project with the Jewish National and University Library.

Microforms have been helpful to the Judaica Division in acquiring theses and dissertations in Jewish Studies from institutions in the United States, Canada, France, Poland, and especially Israel. Many of these dissertations are either never published or appear only many years later. The Division has acquired over 4,000 Israeli doctoral and masters dissertations produced chiefly at the Hebrew University, Tel Aviv University, Bar-Ilan University, and University of Haifa, as well as over 2,500 dissertations produced at American and Canadian universities in the field of Jewish Studies.

The Division has also been able to acquire collections of Jewish archival holdings in microform, including the archive of the underground group Irgun Zvai Leumi in Mandate Palestine; archives chiefly from Eastern Europe dealing with the Holocaust, from the United States Holocaust Memorial Museum, which microfilmed these materials in their original locations; the archive of the leading French Jewish organization, the Alliance Israélite Universelle; archival materials on Jews in England, France, Germany, Italy, and the Netherlands, from the eighteenth to the twentieth centuries; Jewish theater in the nineteenth and twentieth centuries; U.S. State Department records on Palestine in the 1930s and 1940s. In addition to archival materials, the Division has acquired microfilmed collections of printed materials such as eighteenth-century Anglo-Jewish pamphlets, early Hebrew books, and Yiddish books.

The Division has been able to amass a substantial collection of Hebrew manuscripts on microfilm: Hebrew manuscripts from the Jewish Theological Seminary of America (New York); Hebrew manuscripts from the Hebrew University Library (Jerusalem); Hebrew manuscripts from libraries in St. Petersburg and Moscow.

These microforms are copies of materials in libraries and archives throughout the world—Jewish National and University Library, Library of Congress, New York Public Library, Hebrew Union College (Cincinnati), Jewish Theological Seminary of America (New York), Leo Baeck Institute

(New York), YIVO Institute (New York), Alliance Israélite Universelle (Paris), Oriental Institute of the Academy of Science (St. Petersburg), Russian State Library (Moscow), the Academy of Sciences (Bucharest), the Jewish Historical Institute (Warsaw), the Polish National Library (Warsaw), and various archives in Eastern Europe microfilmed by the United States Holocaust Memorial Museum—to name some of the institutions that are the source of substantial bodies of microfilmed materials acquired. In this way, vast amounts of research materials in other libraries and archives have become an integral part of Harvard's Judaica library resources and thus available to all who use the Harvard Library. In the same manner, many Judaica books, pamphlets, and periodicals that have been microfilmed by Harvard have been acquired from Harvard by others, and thus have become part of Judaica library collections throughout the world.

Sound Recordings

The sound recordings in the Judaica Collection number some 28,000 titles (11,000 on compact disc, 8,600 on cassette, 8,400 on sound disc)—of which 22,000 titles are in Hebrew. These sound recordings are of two kinds: music—both Jewish and Israeli—and spoken word, dealing with Jewish history, Judaism, Hebrew literature, and Israel. The collection of Jewish music recordings includes sound discs (33, 45, 78 rpm), cassette tapes, and compact discs. The Judaica Division collects recorded Jewish and Israeli music of every type: popular music, synagogue music, *musikah mizrahit* (Israeli Oriental music), folk songs, instrumentals. The majority of the recordings are of Israeli Hebrew popular music, and the collection is rather comprehensive. Not only does it include recordings produced and distributed commercially, but it also has thousands of recordings not available commercially, such as promotional singles (LPs and CDs) produced for use by disc jockeys on Israeli radio programs, as well as a collection of songs commissioned by Kol Yisrael (the Israeli national radio) for use in its programs—the latter recordings preserved on CDs through the efforts of Harvard and the Jewish National and University Library. The Israeli component also includes synagogue music, folk songs, and the ethnic music of Jewish communities that immigrated to Israel.

In addition to music recordings from Israel, the Library has a substantial collection of music recordings from throughout the Jewish world. They include Yiddish songs recorded in the United States, Latin America, Europe, and South Africa. There are also many klezmer recordings. Hebrew liturgical music is especially well represented, ranging from cantors to children's choirs. Recordings of songs of Jewish content are available in a variety of languages besides Hebrew and Yiddish: Ladino, Judeo-Arabic, English, and Spanish, among others. These vary widely in content, ranging from modern Orthodox to "radical Jewish" to Jewish Christian. Jewish children's songs chiefly in Hebrew, Yiddish, and English are also very well represented.

The non-music component includes sound documentaries from Israel and Jewish communities elsewhere: sermons and lectures on Jewish religious law, ethics, and other topics by rabbis and scholars, chiefly in Israel, the United States, France, and Mexico; commentaries on the Bible and Talmud; cabala; Hasidism; and inspirational tapes. These include recordings produced by organizations such as Kol ha-Daf, Makhon la-Hafakat Shiure Torah Muklatim (Jerusalem), Uve-Lekhtekha va-Derekh (Monroe, NY), Association Dvar Torah (Epinay, France) and Bet-Hamidrash Tecamachalco (Mexico City). There are also proceedings of conferences of organizations, such as the Association for Jewish Studies and Torah UMesorah.

Radio programs represent a large sub-collection of the non-music sound recordings. This includes a substantial part of the archive of Aruts Sheva, a right-wing radio station in Israel, with its daily news broadcasts, political and religious commentators, talk shows, and special events programs. There is also a large selection of programs from Kol Yisrael and from Gale Tsahal, including oral histories and interviews with Israeli authors, artists, political figures and a wide range of individuals involved in the establishment and development of the State of Israel. There are numerous programs on the Israeli cultural scene from the Israeli commercial radio station Radios, including local radio programs as well as programs in Russian. There is also a collection of programs of Aruts Kol ha-Neshamah, a religious radio station. The collection has many radio programs from Jewish communities outside Israel: programs on Yiddish and on North African Jewish culture from France; programs on Israel produced by the Israeli Consulate in New York; programs produced in New York by Jews for Racial and Economic Justice; and a collection of programs on Yiddish culture produced in New York by the Yiddish actors Seymour Rexite and Miriam Kressyn.

Videorecordings

Given the significant role of film and video as a medium of cultural expression and of historical documentation, the Judaica Division has been collecting films produced as videotapes, as well as films converted to videotape format, to VCD, and to DVD, that deal with any aspect of Jewish history and culture. This effort has resulted in a comprehensive collection of videorecordings of Jewish content, some 8,500 titles on videocassette (of which 5,300 are Hebrew), 32 on VCD, and a growing number of DVDs, currently 128 titles.

The Judaica videorecording collection has two components: Israeli and non-Israeli. The Israel videorecording materials (chiefly in Hebrew) are the largest part of the Judaica videorecording collection. Many of the Israeli feature films produced are represented. There are documentaries dealing with all aspects of the history and culture of Israel and of the Jewish people throughout the world, produced by independent filmmakers or public bodies. Also present are videos of performances of plays at the major Israeli theaters. There are videos focused on the work of specific organizations, such as the Histadrut labor federation; political parties, especially their election propaganda; and the kibbutz movement. The religious sector is well represented by many videos of sermons and lectures.

There is a very substantial collection of videos produced by and for the various Israeli television channels, including the main government channel (Channel 1), educational television, and the cable channels Keshet, Tel′ad, and Tekhelet (a religious channel). These include dramas, soap operas, documentaries, children's programs, entertainment, programs dealing with contemporary Israeli issues through guest interviews, and commercial advertisements.

Videos produced by the students of Israeli film schools constitute another large body of materials. These include dramas and documentaries, mostly short films, and are chiefly the work of students at Camera Obscura, the Sam Spiegel Film School, the Tel Aviv University Film and Television Department, and Maaleh, a school for religious (Modern Orthodox) filmmakers.

The collection also has a large number of videorecordings produced as documentation and propaganda by various Israeli governmental and quasi-governmental agencies, Zionist organizations, and other Jewish organizations. These are mainly video conversions from the original films in the Spielberg Jewish Film Archive at Hebrew University of Jerusalem, done as a joint project of the Spielberg Archive and the Judaica Division.

The non-Israeli component of the Judaica videorecording collection consists of videos produced primarily in North and South America and Europe dealing with all aspects of Jewish history and culture, chiefly in the Diaspora but also in Israel. These videos include dramas and documentaries produced by independent filmmakers or by organizations, as well as videos of commercial feature films that have significant Jewish content. There are many old Yiddish feature films in video format. The collection also includes videos produced for Jewish television programs: from the United States, religious programs and a series on Israeli culture produced by the Israeli Consulate in New York; from France, a series featuring documentaries and interviews on Jewish life in France and elsewhere; and from Ukraine, two series of programs on Judaism and on Jewish life in Ukraine—one from Odessa and one from Kiev.

As new formats emerge, the Division moves to collect them. These include DVDs from Israel and the United States, which consist of new productions as well as reissues of titles that appeared in videotape format, often with additional material. Another new type of acquisition is exemplified by that of recent productions of feature films on VCDs in the ultra-orthodox Jewish community in Jerusalem.

CD-ROMs

With the advent of the CD-ROM as a medium of publication, the Judaica Division began collecting Judaica issued in this format, and currently holds some 500 titles. Judaica CD-ROMs include databases, such as the Bar-Ilan Responsa Project, providing access to many volumes of responsa literature as well as other rabbinic texts; and Takdin, providing access to Jewish and Israeli legal literature. Other CD-ROMs include encyclopedias and other Judaica reference works, Jewish classical texts, works on Judaism, and Israeli political materials, as well as Israeli and American Jewish juvenile pedagogical titles. The Division has also acquired a small number of software titles on diskette.

Photographs

Documentation of Jewish life in Israel and elsewhere is also provided by photographs (print and digital), and there are over 130,000 of them among the Judaica Collection's holdings. The largest component consists of photographs of Israeli theatrical, operatic, and dance productions, the work of leading Israeli photographers. Among these are photographs by Gérard Allon, primarily on Habimah Theater; Gadi Dagon, primarily on the Cameri Theater, Khan Theater, Gesher Theater, Tsavta Theater, Temuna Theater, Bet Liessin Theater, New Israel Opera, and Bat Sheva Dance Troupe; Eyal Landesman, primarily on the Haifa Municipal Theater, Teatron ha-Sifriyah, Ha-Teatron ha-Arvi Ivri, dance festivals and musicians; and Yosi Tsveker on musicals. Each production is represented by a large number of photographs, often several hundred. In some cases, the photographs are taken by a digital camera and are stored on a compact disc. The works of

Allon, Dagon, Landesman, and Tsveker cover the Israeli cultural scene since the 1980s. The earlier period is represented by the photographs of Yisrael Haramati on the Cameri Theater from the 1960s to the 1980s, as well as by a small collection of theater photographs by other Israeli photographers.

Other aspects of Israeli life represented in the photograph collection are politics (political figures) and entertainment (popular musicians and television personalities), photographed by Gadi Dagon; impromptu scenes of contemporary Israeli life by Alex Levac; and photographs of immigrants to Israel in the 1950s. There are also collections of slides and filmstrips.

Jewish life in the Diaspora is represented by such collections as Holocaust-related photographs (prints and microfiche); Turkish Jews; a French Jewish cemetery; Jewish life in Carpathia in the 1930s; and the Jewish theater from the 1920s to the 1970s. These last consist of a substantial collection of photographs from the archive of the Yiddish actors Joseph Buloff and Luba Kadison Buloff; photographs from the archives of Yiddish actors Jacob Jacobs, Seymour Rexite and Miriam Kressyn, and Pesach Burstein and Lillian Lux Burstein; and photographs of Jewish theatrical productions in the United States, Argentina, and Europe.

There is also an extensive collection of slides produced in the course of the Division's digitizing of its posters and broadsides.

Ephemera

Ephemera—posters, broadsides, and leaflets—has been and continues to be produced in the Jewish world in connection with activities or events. This material is not intended for general distribution, nor is it generally intended to be preserved. The Judaica Collection has an extensive corpus of such materials—over 250,000 items.

The Israeli ephemera holdings include the world's largest collection of Israeli posters—over 100,000. These include political posters from Israeli national and municipal elections; posters from the religious sector, especially the ultra-orthodox; posters from Israeli theatrical productions; music and entertainment posters; cinema posters, both for Israeli films and for foreign films shown in Israel; art gallery posters; commercial advertisements; and national and local government announcements. These Israeli posters are complemented by extensive holdings of Israeli broadsides and leaflets covering the same topics. Many of these were handed out on streets, others sent in mass mailings often viewed by recipients as "junk mail." Most of the ephemera is from the last half-century, but there is material from earlier years.

Announcement of "Knesset 9," an exhibition of ephemera—posters, broadsides, leaflets—from the 1977 Israeli elections for the Ninth Knesset (Parliament). Shown here: Voting slips bearing the symbols of the twenty-two lists of candidates submitted by political parties and coalitions participating in the elections.

Although most of the ephemera is held in its original format, some ephemera has been acquired only in a surrogate photographic format. This was the case with a large proportion of the posters from the ultra-orthodox community in Jerusalem from 1970 through 2000. In other cases, digital copies were made of posters in other libraries, such as the Ha-Shomer Ha-Tsair Archive in Givat Havivah, or of materials held in private hands, such as a collection of posters dealing with the Jewish religious community in the Land of Israel in the 1920s and 1930s. As noted elsewhere, microfilm has also been used to acquire copies of ephemera held by other libraries.

The Judaica ephemera collection also has substantial holdings, both current and retrospective, of posters, broadsides, and leaflets from Jewish communities all over the world, particularly North and South America and Europe. For example, materials from France deal with such matters as the Dreyfus Affair as well as the social and economic life of Jews in Paris in the decades between the two world wars. Italian ephemera includes eighteenth-century broadsides with Jewish communal regulations. A very large body of material covers all aspects of Jewish life in interwar Poland. The refugee Jewish community in China during World War II is represented by a collection of posters of various cultural events. From Latin America, especially Argentina, there is a large collection of ephemera from the early twentieth century to the present.

Just as is the case with ephemera from Israel, ephemera produced by the various Jewish communities must be acquired immediately; and the Judaica Division has a very active collecting program covering North America, South America, and Europe—particularly the United States, Canada, Mexico, Argentina, Brazil, France, England, Germany, the Balkans, Russia, and Ukraine.

In addition to posters, broadsides, and leaflets, the Judaica Collection collects other categories of non-traditional library materials that can also best be described under the category of ephemera. These include Israeli postage stamps and other philatelic materials; educational and religious games, especially those produced for Orthodox Jews in Israel and the United States; Jewish calendars from communities all over the world; postcards, some with portraits of Hebrew and Yiddish authors (produced in Europe before World War II), others from Israel with scenes of Israel; commercial advertising (including product wrappers, labels, and letterheads) produced by Israeli graphic designers; and dust jackets from Israeli books and from Judaica produced elsewhere. Some types of materials collected are not produced on paper. These include medallions of Jewish interest, e.g., commemoratives issued by Israel; coins (ancient and modern, from Israel); and telecards (commemoratives designed by Israeli graphic artists).

Two topics covered in the collection are particularly multifaceted in format and material: Israeli elections and Jewish theater. The collection of Israeli election ephemera includes not only the more conventional materials such as pamphlets, leaflets, posters, broadsides, sound recordings, videotapes and CD-ROMs, but also many items made of plastic and cloth, such as billboards and banners, as well as a large variety of memorabilia, such as hats, memorial candle containers, signs to go on doorknobs, and T-shirts.

The Jewish theater collection similarly contains a wide variety of items in different formats and materials. To cite one example: the Joseph Buloff Jewish Theater Archive includes posters; playbills; newspaper clippings; letters; photographs; typescripts; costumes; sketches and paintings; and awards and plaques.

Manuscripts

In addition to the many Hebrew manuscripts on microfilm—and, in the case of the Hebrew manuscripts of Mantua's Jewish community, on CD-ROMs—the Judaica Collection also has original manuscript materials. These include manuscripts in various European languages dealing with Jewish life in the late Middle Ages and early modern period; manuscripts related to the Dreyfus Affair; Yiddish theater scripts and music; and a collection of some one hundred Hebrew manuscripts, chiefly rabbinic, cabalistic, and liturgical texts. In addition there are manuscript materials in the various theater and literary archives in the Judaica Collection.

Artwork

The Judaica Collection also includes original artwork that documents Jewish life. The largest such collection consists of several hundred sketches, drawings, and paintings by the American Jewish artist Lionel Reiss, who visited Jewish communities in Eastern Europe before World War II and recorded images of Jewish life there, including many portrait studies. There is also a collection of some seventy-five sketches, drawings, and paintings by Avner Katz, leading Israeli book illustrator. These are the originals of illustrations that were printed in Israeli children's books as well as in other books, and they thus provide an opportunity to study Israeli book illustration by comparing the printed version in the book collection to the originals behind the printed version. Also in the collection are drawings and paintings from the world of the Jewish theater: stage sets for Yiddish theater productions in

Argentina (1920s to 1940s), by the Argentine Jewish artist Misha Schwartz; and stage sets and portraits dealing with the careers of Joseph and Luba Kadison Buloff.

Jewish Ceremonial Objects

The Library has a collection of some 166 ceremonial objects presented in 1990 by Dr. and Mrs. Henry J. Tumen. The collection includes Sabbath candlesticks, Hanukkah menorahs, Passover Seder plates, spice boxes, a ketubah (marriage certificate), and a wedding commemorative "papercut" (on parchment).

How the Judaica Collection Was Built

Acquisition by Gift

The Judaica Collection has reached its current size and scope through a combination of gifts and purchases. As noted in Chapter 2, gifts were significant in the early history of the Judaica Collection. Indeed, it was a series of gifts over a quarter of a century that made Harvard's Hebraica Collection into a world-class collection: the Alberts family collection in 1926; a collection of Hebraica given by Julius Rosenwald in 1929; the Deinard Collection, gift of Lucius N. Littauer in 1930; the Fink Collection, gift of Mr. Littauer in 1930; the Enelow Collection, gift of Mr. Littauer in 1937; and the Felix Friedmann Collection, gift of a committee of donors in 1951. The initial step in establishing the eminence of Harvard's Western-language Judaica holdings was a gift (by bequest) of Lee M. Friedman in 1957, while the foundation of Harvard's Yiddish collection consisted of the gifts of Yiddish materials given by Leo Wiener in November 1898 and by Morris Loeb and James Loeb in December 1898.

Gifts of materials have continued to be significant. The Judaica collection was strengthened by the gift of some 2,000 Hebraica and Judaica books from the library of Rabbi Daniel Jeremy Silver (Class of 1948), given by him over the years from 1973 until his death in 1989. The collection included much rare Hebraica as well as Judaica in other languages, sets of Judaica periodicals in various languages, and several Hebrew manuscripts. Additional gifts of books from Rabbi Silver's library were given in 1991 and 1997 by his widow, Adele Silver. Rare Hebrew books and coins from the collection of Michael Zagayski were presented to the Library in 1980 by his widow Doris Zagayski. The bequest of Professor Harry A. Wolfson in 1974 also added many Hebrew titles to the collection. The Yiddish Collection has been enhanced through a number of gifts: books given over many years by A. A. Roback; the Leyzer Ran collection of books and pamphlets, given by his family in 1996; and books from the library of Jacob Pat, presented by his family in 1996. Other areas of the Judaica Collection were also strengthened over the years by gifts. Books from the libraries of Dr. Judah Shapiro (Ed.D. 1959) in 1981 (some 1,600 items) and Rabbi Joseph Shubow (Class of 1920, Ph.D. 1959) in 1971 (some 1,000 items) added titles to a number of areas of the Judaica Collection, including Yiddish and modern Jewish history, especially Zionism. Many large gifts of Judaica books, ephemera, and videotapes were given over the years by The Lucius N. Littauer Foundation.

A series of gifts of books, pamphlets, ephemera, and videotapes from the Israeli Consulates in Boston and New York added much to the Library's Israel holdings. Especially important to the growth of the Collection's Israel component have been gifts of publications—over many years—by various Israeli government ministries and other government bodies (national and local), as well as by individuals. The wide range of government offices represented by these publications includes the following ministries: Agriculture; Education and Culture; Environment; Finance; Foreign Affairs; Health; Housing; Immigrant Absorption; Industry; Interior; Internal Security; Justice; Labor; Science; Tourism; and Transportation. Other government bodies include: the Israeli Police; the Prime Minister's Office; the State Comptroller's Office; the municipalities of Jerusalem, Tel Aviv, and Haifa; and many others. In addition, a collection of some 800 memorial booklets published by Israeli kibbutzim was given to the Library in 1988 by Arye Ben-Gurion of the Inter-Kibbutz Archive for Jewish Festivals in Bet Ha-Shitah, Israel. A comprehensive collection of Israeli postage stamps and other Israeli philatelic materials was the gift of Stephen I. Rudin (Class of 1953) in 2003.

Gifts from leading Israeli graphic designers Raphie Etgar, Dan Reisinger, Shimon Sandhaus, David Tartakover, Yarom Vardimon, and others strengthened Harvard's holdings in the area of Israeli graphic art. Jewish art holdings were enhanced by the gift of a committee of donors in 1971 of a collection of drawings and paintings by Lionel Reiss; in 1996, the Library received additional works by Lionel Reiss including paintings and sketches, as well as biographical material, the gift of Reiss' son, Dr. David Reiss (Class of 1958). In 1988, Israeli artist Avner Katz gave a collection of his drawings. Dr. and Mrs. Henry J. Tumen gave a collection of Jewish ceremonial objects in 1990.

Gifts have been especially significant in developing the Judaica Collection's holdings of specialized archives. Yiddish Studies, especially

Yiddish theater, was substantially strengthened by a number of gifts: the Joseph Buloff Jewish Theater Archive, gift of his widow the actress Luba Kadison Buloff and daughter Barbara Buloff in 1986, with additions in subsequent years; Jacob Jacobs' Yiddish theater archive, gift of his grandchildren Melanie Mintz and Barry Mintz in 2000; the archive of Yiddish performers Seymour Rexite and Miriam Kressyn, gift of Seymour Rexite in 2001; Yiddish actor Jack Rechtzeit's archive, gift of Frances (Mrs. Jack) Rechtzeit in 2002; and materials from the archive of Yiddish actors Pesach Burstein and Lillian Lux Burstein, gift of Lillian Lux Burstein in 2003. The above-mentioned Leyzer Ran Collection also included Mr. Ran's scholarly archive in the area of Yiddish Studies. The archive of A. A. Roback, received in 1965 by bequest, included considerable correspondence between Roback and Yiddish writers.

The Israel collection was enhanced by receipt of a number of archives: an archive of Israeli radio scripts by Michael Ohad, gift of his family in 2002; an archive of Israeli literary works in English by Zygmunt Frankel, gift of his widow, Alona Frankel, in 2002; and a collection of tapes and transcripts of an oral history of the Israel Philharmonic Orchestra, gift of the Orchestra in 1996.

American Jewish history holdings were strengthened by the Littauer Foundation's gifts of the papers of Lucius N. Littauer and of the Foundation's long-time president, Harry Starr (Class of 1921, LL.B. 1924), as well as a microfilm copy of the papers of Abba Hillel Silver, Reform rabbi and Zionist leader. The Library also received by bequest the papers of Professor Wolfson, with much material on his work and long career at Harvard.

Gifts of individual items, or small batches of materials, have also significantly enriched the Judaica Collection. Examples include a Hebrew prayerbook, Roman rite, printed in Venice in 1588, gift of a Harvard University administrator from her grandfather's collection; books contributed by a scholar to fill gaps detected in the holdings of the Holocaust collection; ephemera related to the Orthodox Jewish community in New York, gift of a book dealer in religious Hebraica Americana; Israeli Hebrew children's books, from the family of the author; privately printed Israeli memorial volumes, sent by the families or organizations publishing them; a collection of Jewish literary works in Romanian published in Israel and Romania, gift of an Israeli Zionist leader originally from Romania; textbooks used in American Jewish religious schools, gift of an alumnus; organizational publications, sent as gifts by organizations such as the American Jewish

Committee, American Jewish Joint Distribution Committee, Union of Orthodox Jewish Congregations of America, and Agudath Israel of America; a file of New Jersey Jewish newspapers, gift of the publisher; Australian Jewish ephemera, sent by an alumnus residing in Australia; German Jewish ephemera, sent by scholars and librarians in Germany; ephemera on Israeli culture, gifts of various Israeli artists and writers who send materials that they receive in the mail on various aspects of Israeli culture, such as announcements of art gallery exhibition openings, lectures, or other cultural events; a collection of slides of scenes of Israel, photographed by the donor; American Jewish commemorative medallions, gift of a Harvard professor; LPs, cassette tapes, CDs, and videotapes, the gifts of performers and producers; old Yiddish LPs, gifts of individuals who had such materials in the family for many years; and Jewish music scores and songbooks, gift of an alumnus and his brother from the library of their mother, a musicologist. In addition, the Division has received gifts from various libraries in the United States, Europe, and Israel of duplicates released from their collections.

These gifts—whether individual items or collections of materials—often fill in long-standing gaps, provide materials that would otherwise very likely not be acquired, and contribute much to the growth of the collection.

Acquisition by Purchase

Although gifts of Judaica material have been and continue to be invaluable, critical to the growth of the Judaica Collection has been sustained development of the collection by means of systematic purchase of materials year after year. The Division's emphasis on securing a "critical mass" in "real time" has necessitated programmatic and unrelenting effort on a global basis to assure that currently published Judaica is acquired by the Library, either by the Judaica Division itself in the case of Hebrew script materials and much non-commercially published Judaica in other languages, or by the Library's Collection Development Department in the case of Western-language Judaica available through regular commercial channels.

The pursuit of items to be purchased on an individual basis is very labor-intensive. Fortunately, shortly after the establishment of the Judaica Division, the difficulty in acquiring Israeli Hebrew publications was considerably alleviated when the United States government extended to Israel a book-procurement program that had recently been established through the Public Law-480 Program. This enabled the Library of Congress to purchase in certain countries local publications for distribution to American research libraries. The funds for doing so came from the use of blocked local currency that had accumulated to the credit of the United States from foreign purchases of surplus agricultural products. In 1964, the American Libraries Book Procurement Center of the Library of Congress was set up in Tel Aviv. From 1964 until the demise of the program in 1973, the Center supplied to some two dozen American research libraries—including Harvard—a copy of most monographs and periodicals published in Israel during that period. At the height of the program in 1967/68, participating libraries received that year some 2,600 volumes and 10,000 periodical issues. This program functioned in effect as a blanket-order approval plan, relieving libraries of the need to order items on an individual basis.

When the PL-480 Program was terminated for lack of funds in 1973, the Judaica Division had to develop a strategy to acquire Israeli publications on its own. Initially, individual orders were placed with various vendors, but it soon became clear that this was not effective. Experience with the PL-480 Program had demonstrated the effectiveness of a comprehensive approval plan implemented by a local vendor positioned to know as soon as a publication is available and to acquire it before it goes out of print—the latter increasingly common because of short press runs and limited inventory. The Division engaged the A.I. Weinberg firm, supplier of books and periodicals to the Israel PL-480 Program, and set up a comprehensive approval plan with that firm in 1975. It has continued to the present. This successful strategy with regard to Israeli publications has also been applied to American Hebraica, and specialized religious Judaica in English.

Consultation and cooperation between the Judaica Division and the book selectors in the Library's Collection Development Department assure the acquisition of Western-language Judaica published currently throughout the world as part of the collecting efforts of the Collection Development Department, increasingly through approval plans whose specifications include the comprehensive selection of Judaica. In addition, the Judaica Division employs a variety of other means to pursue individual items; these range from publisher's announcements to postings on Internet web pages of commercial publishers and non-profit organizations, as well as electronic bulletins of special interest groups. The more labor-intensive pursuit of items not available through approval plans is made possible by the time saved in other cases by the use of approval plans. This combination of approval plans and individual selection has enabled the Judaica Division to acquire substantial numbers of publications in all formats—in recent years adding an average of 15,000 Judaica titles per year, not including the many Judaica publications acquired through the Collection Development Department.

The acquisition of large collections was essential to the accelerated development of the Judaica Collection in the first half of the twentieth century. Indeed, as Professor Wolfson noted in his essay *Hebrew Books in Harvard*, reliance on acquiring collections was a deliberate strategy:

> To accomplish this, two ways were open. One was the tedious, expensive, and to us, without an adequate staff to deal with Hebrew books, the impracticable method of searching for books and buying them one by one. The other was to wait for an opportunity when a collection of some magnitude and of some degree of completeness was given to us or purchased for us. We chose to follow the latter method.

However, the larger the Judaica Collection grew over several decades, the less the acquisition of collections became an option because, inevitably, there would be large amounts of duplication. Acquisition on an individual-item basis had to become the norm.

Opportunities do, however, arise to acquire smaller, more focused collections of Judaica, both current and retrospective, which because of their very specialized nature do not duplicate Harvard's holdings and do fill in gaps in the Judaica Collection. Examples of such collections acquired include North African Hebrew and Judeo-Arabic imprints of the late nineteenth and early twentieth centuries, from a North African Hebrew printer; nineteenth-century German pamphlets published in Hungary and dealing with the political emancipation of Hungarian Jewry, from an antiquarian bookseller; local British Jewish theatrical ephemera, from a bookseller; exhibition catalogs and ephemera issued by Israeli art galleries and museums from the 1930s to the 1990s, from an Israeli art historian; a collection of programs of the Israel Philharmonic Orchestra, from a collector; photographs (print and digital) documenting Israeli theater, dance and music, from the archives of Israeli photographers; Israeli radio and television programs, from the archives of the various Israeli broadcasting companies; collections of sound recordings focused on a specific aspect of Jewish life, such as orthodox Judaism, from their producers; large accumulations of Judaica ephemera from Israel and other countries, from various individuals collecting on behalf of the Judaica Division; digital copies of sound collections from the archives of institutions such as the Jabotinsky Institute (Tel Aviv) and Gale Tsahal (Tel Aviv); videotape copies of films from collections such as the Spielberg Jewish Film Archive (Jerusalem); and, of course, many collections of Judaica in microform, described above.

On an individual basis also, the Division acquires much retrospective material—ranging from eighteenth-century and nineteenth-century Hebrew rabbinic texts to nineteenth-century and early twentieth-century Judaica in

European languages to Israeli Hebrew imprints from the 1920s to the 1980s, chiefly from vendors in the United States, Europe, Israel, and Latin America, who offer materials on a reserved basis at a reasonable cost.

Despite considerable retrospective collecting, however, the Division's primary focus is on collecting current materials. Because of this emphasis, the Division is making a unique contribution to scholarship, since the Division has determined that through the amassing of vast quantities of information (the "critical mass") in currently produced materials—particularly those not commercially available and that can be collected only in "real time"—it does not duplicate the strengths of other Judaica collections. The current Judaica materials being acquired by the Division are often quite scarce or rare, in many cases perhaps unique, and will become other generations' rarities.

In this fashion, the Division has tried to realize—for Judaica as well as Hebraica—the hope expressed three-quarters of a century ago by Professor Wolfson in his above-mentioned essay:

> The function of a great university library is twofold, that of a museum and that of a laboratory. In its capacity of a museum, it should harbor every book that is rare and unique and in need of a place where it may be safely kept and be preserved....In its capacity of a laboratory, it should acquire every book that may be helpful to the scholar in his researches or the presence of which may be stimulative to new researches. This is what establishes the position of the Hebrew collection among the books in the College Library, and this may also serve as a guide in its future growth and development.

TABLE 1 – WIDENER LIBRARY MONOGRAPH HOLDINGS BY LANGUAGE

Languages representing more than 1% of total monograph holdings as of November 13, 2003.

Total	**4,421,934**	**100.00%**
English	1,545,829	34.96%
German	629,004	14.22%
French	399,875	9.04%
Spanish	282,351	6.39%
Russian	276,710	6.26%
Italian	223,295	5.05%
Hebrew	**155,782**	**3.52%**
Arabic	139,043	3.14%
Portuguese	68,139	1.54%
Dutch	67,576	1.53%
Polish	63,727	1.44%
375 other languages	567,941	12.84%
Unknown	2,662	0.06%

TABLE 2 – HARVARD COLLEGE LIBRARY HEBRAICA (HEBREW-SCRIPT) MONOGRAPHS BY DATE OF PUBLICATION

Print & microform formats as of October 1, 2003.

	Hebrew*		Yiddish		All Hebrew & Yiddish	
1469-1499	29	0.02%		0.00%	29	0.02%
1500-1599	732	0.45%	16	0.07%	748	0.40%
1600-1699	656	0.40%	23	0.10%	679	0.37%
1700-1799	2,410	1.48%	49	0.22%	2,459	1.33%
1800-1849	2,965	1.82%	79	0.36%	3,044	1.64%
1850-1874	3,052	1.87%	274	1.25%	3,326	1.80%
1875-1899	4,915	3.01%	1,580	7.19%	6,495	3.51%
1900-1909	3,160	1.94%	1,692	7.70%	4,852	2.62%
1910-1919	2,246	1.38%	1,714	7.80%	3,960	2.14%
1920-1929	3,731	2.29%	3,466	15.77%	7,197	3.89%
1930-1939	3,725	2.28%	3,623	16.48%	7,348	3.97%
1940-1949	5,504	3.37%	2,362	10.74%	7,866	4.25%
1950-1959	8,301	5.09%	1,908	8.68%	10,209	5.51%
1960-1969	16,564	10.15%	1,473	6.70%	18,037	9.74%
1970-1979	19,958	12.23%	1,031	4.69%	20,989	11.34%
1980-1989	28,122	17.24%	1,592	7.24%	29,714	16.05%
1990-1999	41,416	25.38%	561	2.55%	41,977	22.67%
2000	4,604	2.82%	42	0.19%	4,646	2.51%
2001	4,348	2.66%	30	0.14%	4,378	2.36%
2002	4,018	2.46%	61	0.28%	4,079	2.20%
2003	1,213	0.74%	24	0.11%	1,237	0.67%
unknown	1,493	0.92%	385	1.75%	1,878	1.01%
Total	**163,162**	**100.00%**	**21,985**	**100.00%**	**185,147**	**100.00%**

	Hebrew*		Yiddish		All Hebrew & Yiddish	
1475-1899	14,759	9.05%	2,021	9.19%	16,780	9.06%
1900-1949	18,366	11.26%	12,857	58.48%	31,223	16.86%
1950-1999	114,361	70.09%	6,565	29.86%	120,926	65.31%
2000-2003	14,183	8.69%	157	0.71%	14,340	7.75%
unknown	1,493	0.92%	385	1.75%	1,878	1.01%
Total	**163,162**	**100.00%**	**21,985**	**100.00%**	**185,147**	**100.00%**

* Of the above "Hebrew" totals, books in Hebrew constitute 162,260, and Ladino, Judeo-Arabic, and Judeo-Persian make up the remaining 902 titles.

Table 3 – Harvard College Library Hebraica (Hebrew-script) Monographs by Country of Publication

Print & microform formats as of October 1, 2003.

	Hebrew	Ladino	Judeo-Arabic	Judeo-Persian	Yiddish	**Total**
TOTAL	**162,260**	**681**	**192**	**29**	**21,984**	**185,145**
Israel	**125,306**	**108**	**16**	**23**	**2,194**	**127,646**
United States	**12,476**	**27**	**8**	**2**	**6,654**	**19,167**
New York	10,780	8			6,014	**16,802**
Michigan	419	1	7	2	22	**451**
New Jersey	385				30	**415**
Illinois	86				216	**302**
Pennsylvania	151		1		110	**262**
California	84	11			136	**231**
Massachusetts	118	1			37	**156**
Ohio	125	4			18	**147**
Missouri	119				9	**128**
Maryland	66				12	**78**
Connecticut	37				7	**44**
District of Columbia	19				15	**34**
Florida	23				11	**34**
15 other states	64	2	0	0	17	**83**
Europe, Eastern	**10,435**	**30**	**0**	**0**	**8,702**	**19,167**
Belarus	169				285	**454**
Bulgaria	8	14			2	**24**
Estonia					2	**2**
Latvia	34				104	**138**
Lithuania	1,711				1,986	**3,697**
Moldova	17				23	**40**
Poland	5,263				3,785	**9,048**
Romania	324				145	**469**
Russia	144				1,236	**1,380**
Ukraine	2,746				1,130	**3,876**
Yugoslavia, Former	19	16			4	**39**

Table 3 continued

	Hebrew	Ladino	Judeo-Arabic	Judeo-Persian	Yiddish	Total
Europe, Western	**4,815**	**161**	**15**	**0**	**1,057**	**6,048**
Belgium	116				18	**134**
Cyprus	1					**1**
Denmark	18				17	**35**
Finland	1				1	**2**
France	304		4		485	**793**
Greece	411	117			6	**534**
Ireland	8					**8**
Italy	1,698	31	7		13	**1,749**
Netherlands	910	1	1		34	**946**
Portugal	9				1	**10**
Spain	24	11				**35**
Sweden	19				6	**25**
United Kingdom	1,296	1	3		476	**1,776**
Europe, Central	**4,731**	**49**	**1**	**1**	**577**	**5,359**
Austria	874	44	1		91	**1,010**
Czechoslovakia, Former	626	1			28	**655**
Germany	2,697	2		1	386	**3,086**
Hungary	438	1			28	**467**
Switzerland	96	1			44	**141**
Latin America	**542**	**6**	**1**	**0**	**1,747**	**2,296**
Argentina	422	4	1		1,484	**1,911**
Bolivia	2					**2**
Brazil	47				37	**84**
Chile	3				10	**13**
Colombia	4				2	**6**
Cuba					31	**31**
Mexico	40	1			119	**160**
Uruguay	23	1			64	**88**
Venezuela	1					**1**

Table 3 continued

	Hebrew	Ladino	Judeo-Arabic	Judeo-Persian	Yiddish	Total
Middle East/North Africa	**1,541**	**257**	**143**	**2**	**3**	**1,946**
Algeria	58		7			**65**
Egypt	110	23	1		3	**137**
Iran	8			1		**9**
Iraq	106		16	1		**123**
Lebanon	7					**7**
Libya	6					**6**
Morocco	96		13			**109**
Syria	38		4			**42**
Tunisia	633		99			**732**
Turkey	468	234	1			**703**
Yemen	11		2			**13**
Australia/Canada	**220**	**0**	**0**	**0**	**326**	**546**
Australia	17				62	**79**
Canada	203				264	**467**
Far East	**94**	**0**	**8**	**0**	**4**	**106**
China	16				4	**20**
India	78		8			**86**
Africa	**25**	**0**	**0**	**0**	**66**	**91**
Kenya	1					**1**
South Africa	24				66	**90**
Unknown	**2,075**	**43**	**0**	**1**	**654**	**2,773**

Table 4 – Israel Imprints – Harvard College Library Hebraica (Hebrew-script) Monographs by Date of Publication

Print & microform formats as of November 13, 2003.

	Hebrew*		Yiddish		All Hebrew & Yiddish	
1563-1599	4	0.00%	0	0.00%	4	0.00%
1800-1849	39	0.03%	0	0.00%	39	0.03%
1850-1874	81	0.06%	0	0.00%	81	0.06%
1875-1899	321	0.25%	1	0.05%	322	0.25%
1900-1909	512	0.41%	1	0.05%	513	0.40%
1910-1919	360	0.29%	5	0.23%	365	0.28%
1920-1929	1,220	0.97%	33	1.54%	1,253	0.98%
1930-1939	2,292	1.82%	80	3.74%	2,372	1.85%
1940-1947	3,186	2.52%	51	2.39%	3,237	2.52%
1948-1949	1,017	0.81%	29	1.36%	1,046	0.81%
1950-1959	6,980	5.53%	157	7.34%	7,137	5.56%
1960-1969	15,071	11.94%	497	23.25%	15,568	12.13%
1970-1979	18,356	14.54%	522	24.42%	18,878	14.70%
1980-1989	25,309	20.05%	386	18.05%	25,695	20.01%
1990-1999	37,015	29.32%	274	12.82%	37,289	29.04%
2000	4,091	3.24%	13	0.61%	4,104	3.20%
2001	3,867	3.06%	6	0.28%	3,873	3.02%
2002	3,723	2.95%	31	1.45%	3,754	2.92%
2003	1,507	1.19%	27	1.26%	1,534	1.19%
unknown	1,304	1.03%	25	1.17%	1,329	1.04%
Total	**126,255**	**100.00%**	**2,138**	**100.00%**	**128,393**	**100.00%**

	Hebrew*		Yiddish		All Hebrew & Yiddish	
1563-1899	445	0.35%	1	0.05%	446	0.35%
1900-1947	7,570	6.00%	170	7.95%	7,740	6.03%
1948-1999	103,748	81.37%	1,865	87.23%	105,613	82.26%
2000-2003	13,188	10.45%	77	3.60%	13,265	10.33%
unknown	1,304	1.03%	25	1.17%	1,329	1.04%
Total	**126,255**	**100.00%**	**2,138**	**100.00%**	**128,393**	**100.00%**

* Of the above "Hebrew" totals, there are 126,113 in Hebrew; books in Ladino, Judeo-Arabic, and Judeo-Persian make up the remaining 142 titles.

Table 5 – Hebrew Printed Books by Subject

Includes books in Widener, Houghton, and Government Documents, as of November 16, 2003.

TOTAL Hebrew Printed Books	**161,542**	**100.00%**
Rabbinic Literature	**57,932**	**35.86%**
Bible	8,838	5.47%
Cabala & Hasidism	5,711	3.54%
Codes	9,203	5.70%
Ethics	3,397	2.10%
Homiletics	3,311	2.05%
Liturgy	8,664	5.36%
Midrash	538	0.33%
Mishnah	782	0.48%
Philosophy & Theology	5,521	3.42%
Responsa	3,410	2.11%
Talmud	8,557	5.30%
Hebrew Language and Literature	**39,144**	**24.23%**
Hebrew Children's Literature	12,471	7.72%
Hebrew Language	3,272	2.03%
Hebrew Literature	23,401	14.49%
Jewish Social Sciences and Arts	**43,094**	**26.68%**
Diaspora	8,863	5.49%
Israel - Archaeology	149	0.09%
Israel - Arts	2,141	1.33%
Israel - Biography	3,254	2.01%
Israel - Economics	2,641	1.63%
Israel - Education	2,859	1.77%
Israel - Geography	748	0.46%
Israel - Government	2,637	1.63%
Israel - Government Documents	872	0.54%
Israel - History	9,895	6.13%
Israel - Intellectual life	428	0.26%
Israel - Jerusalem	912	0.56%
Israel - Kibbutz	1,064	0.66%

TABLE 5 CONTINUED

Jewish Social Sciences and Arts (continued)		
Israel - Law	872	0.54%
Israel - Local History	75	0.05%
Israel - Military Affairs	455	0.28%
Israel - Music	204	0.13%
Israel - Religion	449	0.28%
Israel - Religion	449	0.28%
Israel - Sciences	723	0.45%
Israel - Sociology	1,804	1.12%
Israel - Tel Aviv	532	0.33%
Zionism	1,517	0.94%
Non-Judaica in Hebrew	**16,000**	**9.90%**
Non-Judaica in Hebrew - Humanities (except Literature)	3,617	2.24%
Non-Judaica in Hebrew - Literature	6,974	4.32%
Non-Judaica in Hebrew - Science	3,235	2.00%
Non-Judaica in Hebrew - Social Sciences	2,174	1.35%
Not Available*	**5,372**	**3.33%**

* This report was based on a statistical analysis of call numbers. For technical reasons it is not possible to automatically extract subject categories from a few call number types.

Chapter Four

Making Harvard's Judaica Collection Accessible

The Judaica Division has over the past forty years aimed to maximize access to Harvard's Judaica holdings. The Division has done so, above all, by utilizing efficient and cost-effective cataloging. It has also sought to maximize access by preservation and collection management strategies and the innovative use of new technologies. The Division has offered reference service and research guidance and has maintained an extensive outreach program of publications, exhibitions, lectures, and conferences. Division staff have participated in professional library activities on the national and international scene and have fostered contact between the Judaica Division and the scholarly community. All of this was done—and continues to be done—with the goal of enhancing access to the Harvard Judaica Collection.

Providing Access through Cataloging

The entire holdings of the Harvard Judaica Collection are listed in HOLLIS, the online catalog of the Harvard University Library, and this catalog's bibliographic records—including those for Harvard's Judaica—are freely accessible via the Internet from any computer anywhere in the world. This section describes how Harvard's Judaica records came to be so widely accessible a resource to scholars.

From the earliest days of the College Library, Harvard's Judaica materials have been recorded in the Library's catalogs. Until the mid-nineteenth century, these catalogs were themselves books, sometimes in manuscript and sometimes in printed form. Subsequently, records for Judaica were also incorporated in the Library's card catalog, which began in 1862. And just as Judaica was integrated into the catalog, so were the books physically incorporated into the Library's regular classification, which meant that they were shelved initially with Biblical Studies and later—as the number of Judaica books increased—throughout the Library in virtually all the classes, e.g., books on Jews in France were shelved in Fr (French history).

In the 1930s, a Judaica classification scheme (Jud) was devised by the Library with the assistance of Professor Wolfson. This was to implement the plan referred to in Library Director Blake's November 23, 1929, letter to Mr. Littauer: "We are just laying out plans to form a comprehensive Jewish collection from the other classifications in our Library and to make it into one of the main groups of books." Professor Blake also made explicit the reason for this: "In doing this, we are but recognizing the intellectual and spiritual unity which characterizes the literary monuments of the Jewish people." Although the Jud class provided a centralized shelf location for much of the European-language Jewish historical materials as well as texts and studies in classical Jewish literature, much Judaica continued to be classed and shelved elsewhere. Biblical texts and studies were classed in the Bible class. Literary works with Jewish themes were classed with the national literature in that language: thus, Israel Zangwill in English Literature and Edmond Fleg in French Literature. Many works of local Jewish history were also still classified as subsets within the country classes, such as Br, Fr, and Ger, rather than in the Jud class—probably a reflection of differences in interpretation by individual catalogers. Moreover, newly published volumes of Jewish periodicals that had originally been classed outside the Jud scheme continued to be added to their original location, for example, *American Jewish Year Book* in the US class. Similarly, many monograph series in various areas of scholarship include from time to time monographs dealing with a Jewish topic, and these Judaica monographs were kept with the general series.

This system remained in effect until 1975 when the Library adopted the Library of Congress (LC) classification, the system used by most American research libraries. Adopting the LC system resulted, in effect, in two collections: pre-1976 acquisitions classed and shelved according to the "Harvard system," subsequently called OW, for "Older Widener"; and post-1976 acquisitions classed and shelved according to WID-LC, for "Widener-Library of Congress." Western-language Judaica was henceforth classed in the WID-LC section, which meant that these Judaica publications were dispersed over the entire range of the Library's LC classification system, for example, Jewish history in DS, Jewish religion in BM, Jewish literature in various areas of P, etc.

The problem of interfiling cataloging records for Hebraica, that is, materials in the Hebrew alphabet, could be overcome on an *ad hoc* basis when the numbers were very small; but once the Library's collection of Hebraica had grown to some 15,000 volumes, as it did in the early 1930s, recording Hebraica in the Library's card catalog posed a major problem since it was a Latin-alphabet catalog. Because the traditional method of recording Hebraica in catalogs was by Hebrew title in the Hebrew alphabet, the Library established a separate Hebrew card catalog in the Hebrew alphabet. This consisted chiefly of cards arranged by title, with several trays of cards arranged by author (in Hebrew) for selected works. Originally handwritten, cards were later produced by a manual Hebrew typewriter. There was also a Hebrew shelflist catalog, which was an inventory of the books by call number. The cards for the original Hebrew shelflist were prepared by hand in the early 1930s by a team of students headed by one of Professor Wolfson's students, Samuel Kurland (Class of 1925, Ph.D. 1929). Over the next thirty years, typed Hebrew catalog cards were produced and filed by students and other staff under the direction of the Library's regular catalogers.

As mentioned earlier, in 1960 the Library invited Shlomo Shunami of the Jewish National and University Library to spend a year at the Harvard Library to advise regarding the Hebrew Collection. To bring the Library's Hebrew Catalog into greater conformity with American research library practice, Shunami converted the Hebrew catalog from a Hebrew title main entry catalog to an author main entry catalog, with the author's name given in the Latin alphabet. However, the descriptive cataloging elements remained in Hebrew in accordance with standard research library practice at the time. He also set up a supplementary selected title catalog in Hebrew as well as a selected subject catalog with standard LC subject headings in English. The Yiddish Catalog, originally an author main entry catalog in Yiddish, was similarly converted to one with author main entries and selected subject entries in the Latin alphabet, with a selected title catalog in Yiddish. Both the Hebrew and Yiddish catalogs were still kept as separate entities and not as part of the Library's regular card catalog, so readers had to go to the area adjacent to the Judaica Division to consult them. For the next twenty years or so, this was the form that the Library's Hebrew and Yiddish catalogs retained, with minor improvements in card format in later years due to the use of an electric Hebrew typewriter and eventually in 1977 a bilingual Hebrew-English electric typewriter.

Hebrew-script publications (chiefly Hebrew and Yiddish) also fared quite differently from Western-language Judaica in terms of classification. Before the addition of collections of Hebraica beginning in the 1920s, the small number of Hebrew books in the College Library had been classed with their

European-language counterparts in various parts of the Harvard classification. The growth of the Hebraica Collection to some 15,000 volumes in 1930 necessitated the development of a suitable classification. Recognizing the advantage for both library and reader of keeping all Hebraica together, the Library with Professor Wolfson's assistance devised the Heb and Y classification schemes that would do that. These Heb and Y classifications—revised from time to time—were used to classify Hebrew and Yiddish publications until 1976 when the Library adopted the Library of Congress (LC) classification. At that point new Hebrew and Yiddish acquisitions were classified by the LC scheme, except that the policy of keeping the Hebrew and Yiddish books together by language was maintained. This was done by setting up the WID-LC HEBREW and WID-LC YIDDISH classes, within which the books were classed by the LC classification. The Judaica Division continued to use this system until 1983.

The use of LC was, it gradually became clear, not suitable for the particular circumstances of Hebraica cataloged by the Judaica Division, since a major premise behind the Library's adoption of the LC classification was not valid in the case of Harvard's Hebraica. One of the purposes in adopting the LC scheme had been to facilitate assigning call numbers, the idea being that the availability of large quantities of cataloging data through the national cooperative cataloging effort would eliminate the work needed to determine a call number in many cases. Although this assumption was valid for a large part of the Library's acquisitions, it was not so for Hebraica. The cataloging backlogs of most Judaica collections meant that the Judaica Division could not find enough cataloging copy produced elsewhere to meet its growing needs. As the Judaica Division increasingly acquired materials not being obtained by other libraries, the lack of cataloging copy became even greater. As a result, Division staff itself had to assign call numbers for most of its Hebrew acquisitions. Deriving such classification numbers from a classification manual that then occupied some two shelves was a very time-consuming task that threatened the Division's ability to process Hebraica acquisitions in a timely manner. As a result, the Library approved the Division's proposal to use simplified versions of the original "Older Widener" Hebrew and Yiddish classifications in place of the LC classification for books in those languages.

In these two new classifications, now known as the "Heb 40000" and "Y 10000" minimal classification schemes, books were added in accession sequence to a small number of base numbers. Classification, hitherto time-consuming, became a very quick and relatively simple task. This system also had the advantage of adding all new publications on a topic in chronological order, thus facilitating access to new publications, which were then always grouped together rather than dispersed as in the traditional alphanumeric order.

The new classification system later proved very helpful in terms of management of stack space, since it made possible the efficient transfer of older acquisitions to remote storage in order to make space for new ones. In addition, adding the shelf number by accession provided instant information regarding the rate of growth of each area, and this facilitated space planning in the stacks for Hebraica.

A revolutionary change in Hebrew cataloging began in 1982 with the introduction of computerized cataloging in the Library's Judaica Division, through the Division's participation in the Library's Distributable Union Catalog (DUC). The DUC was a microfiche catalog containing computerized cataloging data produced by the Library's cataloging operations. The DUC made the records for all current acquisitions at Harvard available throughout the University for the first time, wherever there was a fiche reader and copy of the DUC; and, of course, it included records for Judaica in Western languages. However, the computer systems then used at Harvard, as in other university libraries, were able to display data only in the Latin alphabet, and thus could not include records in the Hebrew alphabet. To be included, Hebrew records would have to be romanized (transliterated into the Latin alphabet).

Computerization and the romanization it entailed posed a dilemma for the Judaica Division. If automating the Harvard Judaica Collection's Hebrew cataloging data were to wait until the Harvard online catalog was able to support the Hebrew script, this would mean that access to this collection would have to remain in card catalog form for the foreseeable future (as it turned out, for some two decades). However, the advantages of the new technology were evident, as was the central role the new automated catalog would play in the Library. Therefore, it became increasingly clear to the Judaica Division that automation was a vital necessity if the Hebraica Collection were to move forward with the rest of the Library. The only way to do this was to transliterate the Hebrew cataloging data into the Latin alphabet, for only then could it be input into the Library's computerized cataloging system.

Implementing romanization was no small matter, and indeed was a controversial step for the Judaica Division. Hebrew catalogs had traditionally utilized the Hebrew alphabet. Most Judaica librarians opposed adopting romanization as the means to achieve automation. For some it was a matter of ideology or institutional culture. Others were concerned about the difficulty of romanizing Hebrew data. Since Hebrew was usually written without vowels, romanization required virtually fluent knowledge of Hebrew and an excellent grounding in Hebrew grammar. Therefore, Judaica librarians called for the development of automated systems able to utilize Hebrew alphabet data, and they expressed a determination to delay automating their Hebrew catalogs until such a system would be available. However, the Judaica Division had already concluded that automation was a strategic necessity; and if automation meant romanization, the Division would romanize its Hebrew cataloging data. Thus, in April 1982, the Judaica Division adopted computerized cataloging in romanization for the cataloging of all Hebrew alphabet materials (Hebrew, Yiddish, Ladino, Judeo-Arabic and several other "Judeo-" languages). It was in the microfiche DUC that the computerized romanized Hebrew data first appeared, integrated with the rest of the Library's cataloging data.

Utilizing computerized romanized Hebrew in the DUC was the first in a series of steps that would enable the Division to maximize benefit from the use of new technology. Another such step was the decision to input the romanized Hebrew cataloging data via the local Harvard computer system ("local MARC"—local Machine Readable Cataloging) rather than via the OCLC national utility. Computerized cataloging at Harvard, and elsewhere at that time, meant that the cataloging data was entered first in the national utility's database through a terminal connected directly to the utility, whence it was subsequently downloaded to the local database. Inputting via the local system, however, was simpler and faster and thus enabled the Division to achieve greater productivity, which meant more timely access by patrons to newly acquired materials.

When "local MARC" was discontinued in mid-1985, the Division continued to catalog Hebraica in the new local system, HOLLIS (the Harvard OnLine Library Information System), which began operating on July 1, 1985. However, cataloging data produced via HOLLIS rather than a national utility was considered "provisional," since HOLLIS was then only an online acquisitions system, and it did not provide a cataloging mode. That meant the system did not provide for subject entries, and therefore Hebraica processed in HOLLIS at that time could not have subject headings. However, the Division continued, despite this drawback, out of a conviction that greater productivity and hence reader access to more materials justified using the local system as a catalog. In 1988, cataloging in the local system was adopted by the Library as a cataloging option, and locally entered records could receive all of the cataloging fields required for full "standard" cataloging. In particular, this meant that subject access could be provided. The Judaica Division then did have to upgrade several years' worth of provisional records, but the use of the local system during this period for cataloging had nonetheless resulted in more Hebraica materials being processed than would otherwise have been possible.

As the Judaica Division vigorously pursued automation for cataloging its ongoing acquisitions, it also recognized that automated Hebrew bibliographic data needed to be provided for the whole Hebraica Collection. Otherwise, as patrons became more dependent on the automated catalogs, the books in the old card catalog would be effectively "hidden." It was increasingly clear that retrospective conversion—"recon" in librarian's parlance—of the Hebrew and Yiddish catalogs in their entirety was a matter of the highest priority.

Retrospective conversion became possible in September 1983, when The Horace W. Goldsmith Foundation of New York awarded the Judaica Division the first of a five-year series of grants to support the computerization (in romanization) of the Hebrew and Yiddish card catalogs. Since only a small number of romanized Hebrew catalog records were in the national bibliographic databases, the Judaica Division had to carry out the "recon" without being able to download records from elsewhere.

More than 80,000 Hebrew and Yiddish main entry catalog cards had to be romanized, coded appropriately as part of the conversion process, and then keyed in. Thanks to the Goldsmith Foundation grants, the Division was able to hire additional staff, including large numbers of students. With the added staff, an assembly line was set up that reviewed each main entry catalog card, transcribed the Hebrew cataloging data to worksheets in romanized form, and coded the data in accordance with the requirements of the Library's computerized cataloging system. Because of the state of computers at that time, the romanized worksheets were then sent to a data-entry company for keying onto magnetic tape, which could be loaded into the Library's computerized catalog. After the data was entered and printed out, it was then reviewed for accuracy. This "recon" project began in the fall of 1983 and was concluded in the spring of 1988.

The "recon," in romanized form, of the Hebrew and Yiddish catalogs constituted two firsts. It was was the first major research collection at Harvard to undergo a complete retrospective conversion. As a result, the Judaica Division was now well positioned to benefit from ongoing developments in automation at Harvard, while at the same time Harvard scholars and students no longer needed to consult a card catalog for the older part of the collection.

Nationally, the "recon" of Harvard's Hebrew and Yiddish catalogs was the first at any major Judaica research collection to be completely carried out. Benefits were likewise twofold: to libraries and to scholars directly. In May 1988, Harvard presented tapes of the Hebrew and Yiddish "recon" data to the OCLC and RLIN utilities at a conference arranged at Harvard by the Judaica Division on the topic "Judaica Librarianship: Facing the Future." Making these records available through OCLC and RLIN made it possible for libraries anywhere to use these records in their own cataloging. They could even carry out retrospective conversion themselves—relatively easily, and at substantial cost savings. At the same time, scholars everywhere now had access to Harvard's Hebrew and Yiddish computerized catalog records via OCLC and RLIN, as well as through HOLLIS when the latter became available for public access.

Harvard's contribution of its romanized Hebrew and Yiddish cataloging data to RLIN took on added importance when RLIN developed Hebrew script capability. This was because RLIN's system required a romanized base record to which parallel fields in Hebrew script were then added. Since it was romanization that posed difficulties, libraries could be spared the necessity of having to do the romanization themselves, because usually a romanized Hebrew Harvard record was already in the database.

Despite having the possibility of automated Hebrew and Yiddish records in both the Hebrew and Latin alphabets, the Judaica Division continued its policy of using only romanization. To have produced records in both alphabets would have compromised cataloging productivity, because of the time required to add parallel fields in Hebrew script, without any increase in access by readers, since the Hebrew fields could not have been displayed in Harvard's online HOLLIS catalog. Staying with romanization alone has thus enabled the Judaica Division to continue to catalog Hebrew and Yiddish acquisitions promptly after they are received.

With the Library's decision in the year 2000 to adopt the Aleph system for HOLLIS II, the above situation changed. Aleph, a system developed in Israel, can support non-Roman alphabets as well as Chinese, Japanese, and Korean scripts. When support for non-Roman alphabets is implemented, probably in the next year or so, the Judaica Division plans then to add to its romanized records appropriate parallel fields in the Hebrew alphabet. These points of access in Hebrew will be fully accessible to users of HOLLIS, and therefore the additional labor to add them will be justified by the increased access that these will provide to users. The extent of the Division's use of parallel Hebrew fields in cataloging will be determined by the two factors that have always guided the Division's cataloging: effect on productivity and service to readers.

Providing effective intellectual access to the Judaica Collection is of paramount importance to the Judaica Division, and that, above all, means cataloging promptly newly acquired material. "Cataloging on receipt" has long been the policy of the Division. To implement such a policy, the Division's cataloging workflow has, of course, been designed to conform to national standards for machine-readable cataloging (MARC), while within the parameters of those national standards, streamlining its cataloging to make it efficient and cost-effective. Mention has already been made of the special abridged classification scheme adopted for Hebrew and Yiddish materials and of the decision to continue with romanized Hebrew cataloging until such time as this could be done without adverse effect on productivity. At the same time, the Division has not hesitated to add information that is not required, provided that it enhances access for the reader. The prime example of this is that the Division provides access to place of publication by inputting a standardized place of publication field. The Division may be the only Judaica collection that provides access to all Hebrew and Yiddish monographs and serials by place of publication, and it is one of the few units of the Harvard College Library that provides imprint access for much of its materials.

Cataloging Hebraica at Harvard necessarily requires, to a considerable extent, creating a catalog record for a publication for the first time ("original cataloging"), as opposed to downloading one prepared previously by another library ("copy cataloging"). The primary reason for a high degree of original cataloging is that the Judaica Division acquires so much that is not in other libraries. Thus, there is no possibility of finding catalog records in the national databases for a high proportion of its acquisitions, especially government and organizational publications, children's literature, non-classic rabbinic works, and Hebrew translations. Likewise, most of the Hebraica and Judaica sound recordings and videorecordings are not being acquired by other libraries. Even for the genres of publications that are being acquired by other institutions, there is often no available catalog record because of their cataloging backlogs. Original cataloging has in fact been required for 87 percent of Hebrew monograph titles cataloged by the Judaica Division in recent years. If more cataloging copy becomes available, this will free Judaica Division staff time that could then be devoted to dealing with other materials such as ephemera and special collections. For example, Division staff hope that at some point records from the Israeli Aleph national library network can be used for some of Harvard's cataloging; this would provide Hebrew cataloging data, although it would still require the Division's adding roman-script access points. Another possibility being explored is the use of vendor records, i.e., records produced by the Division's primary supplier of Israeli publications.

Because of the ever-increasing flow of materials being acquired, decreasing the amount of original cataloging is of paramount importance. Otherwise, the Division faces two equally unacceptable options—to cut back on acquisitions or to accumulate uncataloged backlogs. Either would be a great disservice to the scholarly community. The Division is committed to maintaining a balanced operation: a comprehensive acquisitions program with all materials accessible to readers. That is why the Judaica Division continues to focus on maintaining a highly efficient cataloging process that will sustain productivity and service.

To maintain efficient cataloging, the Division has also taken a careful look at the steps in cataloging, so as to make creative use of the latest cataloging technology. In particular, this has meant use of macros or their equivalents. At first, with the "dumb terminals" of the late 1980s, this meant programmed function keys that reproduced text strings that assisted in automating the repetitive portions of ordering and payment, of cataloging microfilm holding records, and of adding subject headings. Later, in the DOS and Windows 3.1 environments, this meant implementing true scripted macros, with NewKey. The transition to Windows 95 and Windows NT brought use of Reflection macros. Most recently, this has meant implementing Macro Express in conjunction with Aleph. Macros written by Judaica Division staff are used in every phase of Judaica operations, from cataloging, to acquisitions, to barcoding—over 400 macros in all. For reasons of productivity, ergonomics, and accuracy, the Division tries to assure that staff need not key in a single unnecessary keystroke that could be handled by the computer. On a basic level, this has meant providing staff with drop-down lists of common subject headings, subject heading elements, and notes. The macros have also been used to reproduce the repetitive keystrokes in whole processes, such as importing an OCLC record, deriving an Aleph bibliographic record from another Aleph bibliographic record, updating a holding record and creating a corresponding item record for a book transferred to the Harvard Depository, and creating order and payment records. In the latter case, a process that without macros would take approximately

46 to 85 keystrokes and mouse clicks, in addition to writing down the order number, and the manual recording of statistics, takes only 10 to 19 keystrokes with macros, with no writing down of order numbers or statistics.

Moreover, the Judaica Division has combined use of other technology to leverage further the use of macros. For example, using FileMaker Developer, individual databases were created for staff to use in conjunction with the order/payment macros. During the order/payment process, the basic bibliographic and acquisitions data is trapped by the macros, making it possible to generate cataloging and acquisitions statistics for each staff member at the end of the month by a push of a button. This has replaced manual statistics sheets and time-consuming tabulation at the end of the month. The Judaica Division has also made much use of the Library's reporting system to track and to do quality-control on cataloging and acquisitions. In all cases, the goal has been to provide patrons with access as quickly as possible to as large a number as possible of Judaica materials in all formats and to provide staff with timely and accurate data to evaluate Division operations in order to find ways to enhance the Division's workflow.

This pragmatic client-oriented approach to cataloging has benefited both the Harvard community as well as the broader national and international scholarly community. For the Harvard community, it has meant that new publications are promptly available. For scholars elsewhere who consult HOLLIS, it provides information on these publications in a timely manner. For libraries everywhere, it has meant that Harvard's romanized cataloging data—which is electronically sent by the Library to OCLC and RLIN after the Judaica Division creates a bibliographic record in HOLLIS—is readily available for most current Hebraica that they acquire, and this facilitates the cataloging of Hebraica in these libraries since they are able to utilize Harvard's catalog records instead of creating their own. Thus, with the computerized romanized cataloging data from Harvard's Hebrew and Yiddish "recon" projects and with the prompt cataloging of current Hebraica, Harvard has become the largest provider of romanized Hebrew machine-readable cataloging data to the national bibliographic utilities.

Cataloging of most current non-Hebrew Judaica acquisitions continues to be done by the Library's Technical Services Department as an integral part of the Library's processing of current Western-language acquisitions. However, as the Division over the years has increased its collecting of current non-Hebrew publications that are not available through the regular booktrade distribution channels (e.g., Jewish community publications from around the globe), and as the Division has acquired more older non-Hebrew

Judaica, the Division has assumed responsibility for cataloging these categories of materials, which in recent years have accounted for some 18 percent of the Judaica Division's cataloging.

In addition to reliance on the key role of the Library's Technical Services Department in the processing of most current Western-language Judaica acquisitions, the Division also relies on the work of the Library's Middle Eastern Division and Slavic Division for cataloging Judaica materials in languages for which those divisions are responsible. The Division has also from time to time recruited outside assistance for cataloging materials requiring specialized expertise, such as the Hebrew manuscript collection, cataloged by Mordechai Glatzer from Hebrew University, in 1970/71; the North African Judeo-Arabic collection, cataloged by Assia Neuberg from the Jewish National and University Library, in 1970/71; and the Ladino Collection, cataloged in 1984 by Aron Rodrigue, then a graduate student at Harvard and now a professor at Stanford University.

The Judaica Division also has responsibility for cataloging Hebrew and Yiddish materials added to two departmental libraries that were set up by the Department of Near Eastern Languages and Civilizations in conjunction with the Center for Jewish Studies, primarily for the use of students and faculty in Jewish Studies. One is the Jewish Studies seminar library located in Widener Library. This is focused on medieval and early modern Jewish history and culture and includes books and periodicals, primarily in Hebrew and English. The other is the Yiddish seminar library, located in Vanserg Hall near the Center for Jewish Studies. This is focused on Yiddish Studies and includes books and periodicals in Yiddish. The books in these two libraries are all duplicates of titles in the Judaica Collection. Indeed, most of the books in them were provided on long-term deposit by the Judaica Division from duplicates that it acquired in various gifts. In the case of Yiddish, these included many books from the libraries of Jacob Pat and Leyzer Ran.

Although the "recon" of the Hebrew and Yiddish collections was completed in 1988, the Western-language Judaica cataloged before the advent of HOLLIS remained in card form, since it was integrated with all the Library's holdings in the Library's main card catalog. When in 1996 the Harvard Library completed the "recon" of its entire card catalog, all the catalog records for Judaica in Western languages were automated as an integral part of this "recon" project. The result was that all of the Library's Judaica holdings in all languages were in machine-readable form and accessible online in HOLLIS to everyone via the Internet—the first major Judaica research collection to be fully online and freely accessible.

Providing Access through Collection Management and Preservation

For libraries, issues of physical access are as important as those of intellectual access. Simply put, a catalog of a library is of very little value if the books it records cannot be found when readers seek to consult them. Books have to be safeguarded so that they will be available when needed. Thus security is an essential component of access, which for Judaica materials is especially important because of the rarity of much of the material. For a variety of reasons—particularly the centuries of persecution, above all the Holocaust of World War II—much Judaica published up to the mid-twentieth century in Europe and Asia has become scarce or rare. For many years, most of Harvard's Judaica materials were freely accessible on shelves in the Widener Library stacks. Rare sixteenth-century editions of the Talmud were on the shelf along with twentieth-century Talmud editions, and rare Passover Haggadot often were borrowed for home use at Passover seders. Given the steady rise in value of these increasingly scarce and rare volumes, it was readily understandable that in 1960 Shlomo Shunami, then serving as a consultant to the Library, transferred some two thousand Hebrew books printed in the sixteenth and seventeenth centuries from the Widener stacks to the Library's rare book department, the Houghton Library, which already housed the large body of rare Western-language Judaica received by bequest from the collection of Lee M. Friedman.

Over the next quarter-century the Judaica Division continued to cull from the stacks especially rare items for transfer to Houghton, for deposit in special locked collections, or for storage in the New England Deposit Library, a book warehouse located across the Charles River in Allston. None of these measures fully solved the problem. However, the Harvard Depository (HD), established in 1986, enabled this issue to be properly addressed for the first time. HD, located in Southboro, some thirty miles west of Cambridge, was designed to solve the Library's acute storage space problem. HD features state-of-the-art climate and security control, and it has enormous capacity because additional storage modules can be built as needed (six so far). It became readily apparent to the Judaica Division that HD offered substantial relief to a number of the Division's pressing concerns: space, security, and preservation.

The tremendous proliferation of Judaica publications, especially of Hebrew books in Israel, since the end of World War II had created a serious shelf-space problem in the Jud and Heb sections of the Widener stacks, much as the increase in publishing throughout the world had done in all other subject areas of the Widener stacks. The availability of HD has made it possible to use shelf-space in Widener for heavily used Judaica, particularly the more recent publications, and to utilize HD for low-use, rare, or fragile materials. Moreover, space for new Judaica acquisitions on the Widener shelves could always be made available through a systematic and ongoing process of transfers to HD. At the same time, HD greatly improved security, since there is no on-site public access to the materials in HD. All items have to be requested, and appropriate restrictions on circulation and handling of certain materials can be more easily imposed.

Beginning with the academic year 1989/90, the Judaica Division began to store materials at HD as an integral part of its collection management policy. Since then, the Division has transferred approximately 164,000 Hebrew and Yiddish titles, or 70 percent of the collection. This included some 34,000 titles that constituted 85 percent of the Hebraica holdings published before World War II—the bulk of the rare, scarce, and fragile Hebraica that had long been particularly vulnerable while in the Widener stacks. Also transferred to HD were a substantial portion of the Hebrew children's literature collection, most Hebrew books on non-Judaic topics in the humanities, social sciences, and science, and Hebrew translations.

On an ongoing basis, all acquisitions of older Hebraica are sent to HD, and all acquisitions of currently published Hebraica are reviewed for possible transfer to HD. At present over three quarters of new Hebraica publications are sent to HD. This includes children's literature, translations, most Israeli government reports, and pamphlets. Pamphlets in Hebrew are sent out as collections of individually cataloged items arranged by call number, which serves to group the pamphlets by subject. Western-language Judaica pamphlets are similarly treated, i.e., are individually cataloged in HOLLIS and boxed by language (e.g., French Judaica pamphlets) or by topic (English pamphlets on Zionism). Ephemera, photographs, and most non-print formats (sound recordings, videorecordings, and CD-ROMs)—both Hebraica and Western-language—are sent to HD (except that most current Jewish and Israeli music CDs are deposited in the Loeb Music Library). Current Western-language Judaica acquired through the Library's Collection Development Department and Technical Services Department is similarly routed to the Widener stacks or HD.

In addition to space and security, HD also provides an optimal preservation environment, because its climate control prolongs the life of material stored there. Preservation, like security, is ultimately an access issue, since material that deteriorates to the point where it ceases to be usable by readers is no longer accessible. Most of the Judaica that is on brittle paper is the material that was published from the mid-nineteenth to mid-twentieth centuries. Since the publications of that period have largely been transferred to HD, the HD environment will help to prolong the life of these materials. HD also provides appropriate storage for audiovisual materials, and therefore most Judaica audiovisual materials are stored there.

HD also furthers preservation by enabling the staff to manage access. Fragile and rare Judaica sent to the Harvard Depository is coded so that before being turned over to readers it can be reviewed by Judaica Division staff, who are therefore able to determine whether or not it may be photocopied directly by the patron, by the Library's Imaging Services Department, or, sometimes, not at all. Control over photocopying can prolong the life of materials. In all this, the Judaica Division staff work closely with the staff of the Phillips Reading Room, the Imaging Services Department, the Preservation Department, and the Harvard Depository.

To assure access to the Library's Judaica materials both for the present as well as the future, the Judaica Division has also actively pursued a Judaica microfilming preservation program. From 1978 to 1981, under grants to the Library from the U.S. Department of Education's "Strengthening Research Library Resources Program: Title II-C of the Higher Education Act of 1965," the Judaica Division prepared for microfilming a substantial twenty-year accumulation of Judaica pamphlets. In various languages, and uncataloged, these pamphlets had been virtually inaccessible to scholars. The Library microfilmed Judaica pamphlets under the Title II-C Program in the following categories: Yiddish (4,200); English (3,300); Hebrew (3,000); German (2,000); Spanish (850); Dutch (750); French (600); Slavic (600); Danish (200)—some 15,500 pamphlets. In addition, files of some 200 Hebrew, 40 Yiddish and 40 Western-language Judaica periodicals were microfilmed—some of them substantial, spanning many years. A number of collections of ephemera were also microfilmed under the Title II-C Program: Israeli political ephemera (municipal elections 1950-1978; 1,000 items); other Israeli ephemera (charities: 650 items; non-Zionist orthodox: 600 items; military affairs: 600 items; labor movement: 600 items); French Judaica (4,200 items); and East European Judaica, chiefly in Yiddish, from Poland (2,300 items), Russia (1,000 items), Romania (200 items) and the Baltic states (500 items). To further facilitate access the Judaica Division provided author-title access to all these materials and issued a series of 16 checklists (nos. 1-10 in hard copy; nos. 11-16 in microfiche) listing all the pamphlets microfilmed. The cataloging records for the microfilmed materials were entered into HOLLIS. The original paper copies of the microfilmed pamphlets were stored in HD.

In 1980, the Judaica Division received a grant from The Lucius N. Littauer Foundation to establish the Harvard-Littauer Judaica Endowment for Judaica preservation. The endowment made it possible to continue the Judaica preservation program through microfilming and, in later years, through digital technology. This endowment also provides funds to acquire Judaica preserved by others. In addition, the fund supports Library activities that promote the preservation of Judaica. Thus, the Division held an international conference on October 19, 1981, focusing on preservation microfilming and scholarly research and the context within which Judaica preservation activity takes place. The Harvard-Littauer Endowment also made possible publication of *Guide to Judaica Serials in Microform in the Harvard College Library* (1981) and *Guide to Judaica Microforms in the Harvard College Library* (1988).

The Judaica Division's preservation strategy encourages the participation of others—both commercial firms as well as libraries—in its preservation projects. A major project to film fragile and rare Hebraica in the Harvard Library—Hebrew Books from the Harvard College Library—was carried out by the German publishing firm K. G. Saur from 1985 through 1989. This resulted in the microfilming of some 4,934 Hebrew titles (on 11,453 microfiche) published from the eighteenth through the early twentieth centuries. Titles filmed were selected by the Judaica Division, which also provided all the cataloging data that enabled Saur to publish subsequently a detailed author/title/subject index to the microfiche collection (*Hebrew Books from the Harvard College Library: Index,* 1996). The successful completion of this project was followed by another Saur-Harvard microfilming project, Yiddish Books from the Harvard College Library, which began in 1990 and was completed in 2000. Some 2,603 Yiddish titles selected by the Judaica Division were filmed (on 5,229 microfiche).

Beginning in 1991, the Judaica Division initiated a number of preservation microfilming projects in cooperation with the Jewish National and University Library (JNUL). In each case JNUL's photographic services department did the filming, but the costs were shared by Harvard and JNUL, with each institution receiving a copy of the film. These projects focused on the microfilming of materials not at Harvard and whose texts, for the most part, could then best be preserved in microfilm since the originals were on poor paper. The projects covered the Israeli local press, the kibbutz press, and the early Israeli press, plus Israeli doctoral dissertations and masters theses.

The Israeli local press consists of over two hundred publications, in a variety of formats, published in cities and towns throughout Israel. The kibbutz press, published all over Israel by nearly two hundred kibbutzim, is older, with some of these bulletins going back to the 1920s and 1930s. In both cases, the JNUL collection served as the basis for the microfilming project. For the kibbutz press, JNUL's collection was supplemented by files located in the archives of the different kibbutz movements. Virtually none of these local publications or kibbutz bulletins were previously available at Harvard. The early Israeli press microfilmed in this project consisted of literary, political, and economic journals; and priority was given to titles hitherto lacking from the Judaica Collection. In addition, the JNUL took responsibility for the ongoing microfilming of later issues of some Hebrew titles microfilmed earlier in the Title II-C Program, and these, too, were microfilmed as a joint project. The JNUL's reference collection of Israeli dissertations and theses was also filmed because most of these titles were unpublished and on poor paper. Microfilming was then the best way in which these materials could be preserved, and at the same time be made available at Harvard.

The Judaica Division and the JNUL also cooperated in microfilming materials that neither library had. In Romania, JNUL filmed a substantial collection of the Romanian-Jewish press—chiefly in Romanian and Yiddish. In Moscow, JNUL filmed a large collection of Jewish press publications in Yiddish with funds provided by the Littauer Foundation. In both cases, copies of the films were deposited in JNUL and Harvard.

Preservation as a strategy for access took on a new dimension thanks to these projects with the JNUL. Rather than try to acquire certain materials that are very costly, difficult—even impossible—to obtain, or are often fragile to the point that they would require microfilming by Harvard in order to be usable for research, the Division has adopted a strategy of relying on preservation microfilming elsewhere as a means to acquire access to these materials. Other examples are: the microfilming of early German and other European Judaica publications by the Universitätsbibliothek Frankfurt am Main, as part of an exchange project with the Judaica Division under the aegis of the German Resources Project, part of the Global Resources Program sponsored by the Association of American Universities and the Association of Research Libraries; and the microfilming of the archives of the Alliance Israélite Universelle (Paris) as a joint project with the Alliance and the Central Archives for the History of the Jewish People (Jerusalem). In other cases, such as with Yiddish books and periodicals microfilmed by the YIVO Institute or American Jewish newspapers microfilmed by Hebrew

Union College, the Division has been able to acquire materials that had already been microfilmed as part of another library's earlier preservation project. Preservation microfilming by others thus serves to augment access at Harvard to Judaica materials otherwise unobtainable.

The advent of digital technology created new opportunities for the Judaica Division to enhance access to the Library's Judaica holdings. The prime example of this was the Division's digitization in 1994 of its collection of Israeli posters. This collection, at that time some 70,000 posters, posed a problem of access that for many years seemed insurmountable. The size of the posters, the quantity of them, and their fragility made it virtually impossible for readers to consult them, not to mention that it was difficult for the Division to organize them and record them. Digital technology provided an efficient solution, in terms of access and preservation. The Judaica Division outsourced the digitization—to a vendor using Kodak Photo-CD technology—of the Judaica poster collection, which consisted largely of Israeli posters, although it included many from Europe, North America, and South America. (New acquisitions of posters and other ephemera that are digitized are now digitized by digital camera.) Access to images of these materials in high resolution digitized format was then made available through an image database on a computer in the Judaica Division. Digitization made it possible to send the original paper copies to the Harvard Depository where preservation of the originals is assured. The Judaica Division is also using digital technology to preserve fragile audiovisual materials by reformatting sound recordings to CDs and videotapes to DVDs. As in the case of microfilming technology, the Division is also using digital technology to acquire copies of materials in other libraries and archives. The Division's large digital projects have made it a pioneer in Judaica librarianship in the use of digital technology for acquiring, preserving, and enhancing access to Judaica materials.

Because of the great interest generated by the Judaica Division's digital image database, database project manager Violet Gilboa, the Littauer Hebraica Technical and Research Services Librarian in the Judaica Division, was invited to take an increasingly active role in Electronic Imaging & the Visual Arts (EVA)—the leading international organization, based in London, that focuses on electronic imaging of visual materials and that works closely with the European Union (EU) in fostering cultural projects. Gilboa has made presentations at EVA invitational conferences in Glasgow (July 2001), Florence (March 2002, March 2003) and London (July 2002, September 2003). These have covered not only the Division's digitization of

Israeli posters, but also Harvard's digital resources for the study of Israeli opera, and the Division's plans for archiving Israeli Internet websites. In recognition of the Division's work in this area, EVA has enlisted the Judaica Division to assist in facilitating cooperative projects, as noted in the *Proceedings* of an EVA invitational international symposium hosted at Harvard by the Judaica Division (October 2002):

> Because of its work over many years in the comprehensive documentation of Israel and its culture as well as in its documentation of European Jewish culture, Harvard's Judaica Collection is well positioned to play a key role in encouraging relationships among many Israeli and European cultural institutions that may lead to proposals for projects within the EU cultural projects guidelines.

That symposium focused on the theme: "U.S.-Europe-Israel: Cooperation in Culture *x* Technology." This was the first in a series of symposia that the Judaica Division is planning with EVA on the theme of European, Israeli, and American cooperation in culture and technology, to take place at Harvard every third year, alternating with sites in Europe and Israel in years one and two. At the second symposium in this series, in London in September 2003, an EVA-sponsored group interested in documenting Jewish culture in Europe, Israel, and elsewhere through digital technology was organized: Archives, Libraries, Museums—Arts (ALMA), with Violet Gilboa as coordinator; she has also been appointed co-chair of EVA's interfaith working group. The next symposia in the series are scheduled for 2004 in Israel, 2005 at Harvard, and 2006 in Berlin. Through this forum, the Judaica Division is working to encourage the use of digital technology to provide increased access to Jewish cultural materials.

Providing Access through Outreach Programs

Publication of various catalogs has also enhanced access to the Judaica Collection. In 1968, the Library published the card catalog of the Hebrew Collection; the six-volume catalog consisted of photographic reproductions of the catalog cards. A three-volume supplement, published in 1972, reproduced catalog cards for Hebraica cataloged between 1969 and 1972. The next published catalog of the Hebrew Collection reflected the advances in technology over the ensuing two decades. In 1995, the Judaica Division published through the K. G. Saur firm an eleven-volume catalog of the Hebrew Collection; it was produced from the computerized romanized Hebrew cataloging records in HOLLIS. In addition to author/title and subject indexes, this catalog also provided access by imprint, in effect providing the first imprint catalog for Hebraica on such a large scale. This was made possible by the Judaica Division's previously mentioned cataloging practice of providing access by place of publication to all Hebrew-script publications.

Similarly, publications have provided enhanced access to other parts of the Judaica Collection. In 1971, the Library published *Judaica*, a catalog of Western-language Judaica in the Jud classification. This was a product of the Library's initial automation project—the computerization of the Library's old shelflist records—and it appeared as volume 39 in the Widener Shelflist Series. The volume also included Judaica housed in the Library's rare book department, the Houghton Library. In addition, the 1972 supplement to the 1968 printed Hebrew catalog included an appendix with reproductions of catalog cards of Western-language Judaica in the Houghton Library and an index to the Houghton Judaica by place of publication.

Access has also been provided to other parts of the Judaica Collection through published catalogs, including *Hebrew Manuscripts in the Houghton Library* (1975), *Guide to Judaica Serials in Microform* (1981), *Guide to Judaica Microforms* (1988), *Guide to Judaica Videotapes* (1989), *Guide to Ladino Materials in the Harvard Library* (1992), *Judaica Sound Recordings* (1996), and *Local Press in Israel* (1996). (For a complete list of Judaica Division publications, see Appendix A.)

Exhibitions, lectures, and conferences have also been part of an overall strategy to enhance access by bringing the Library's Judaica resources to the attention of Harvard faculty and students as well as the national and international community of scholars. (For a complete list of Judaica Division exhibitions, lectures, and conferences, see Appendices B-D.) Since 1968, the Division has arranged some ninety exhibitions. Topics were chosen especially to cover broad areas of Jewish culture, in many cases those in which the Library has materials not readily available elsewhere. These included exhibitions of French Judaica (1972), Russian Judaica (1980), Polish Judaica (1981), the Jewish press (1985), Jewish music (1985), Yiddish theater (1987, 2002), Hungarian Judaica (1987), Italian Judaica (1989), Chinese Judaica (1992), the Yiddish Collection (1993), and Zionism (1996). Many of the Judaica Division's exhibitions have focused on specific types of materials such as Passover Haggadot (1970, 1971, 1977, 1979, 1987, 1988, 1989, 1990, 1991), Jewish calendars (1976, 1977, 1978, 1988), Israeli postage stamps (1992), Jewish student newspapers (1972), children's books (1981, 1984), prayerbooks (1982), Hebrew translations (1985), Jewish ceremonial objects (1990), and bindings of Hebrew books (1996). Many of these contained ephemera, but some have made ephemera central: the

ISRAELI

THEATRE

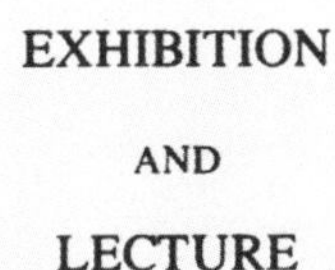

Announcement of exhibition and lecture on the Israeli theater, October 1989. Shown here: playbills of Israeli theatrical productions.

Knesset elections (1977-1978 and 1984), the ultra-orthodox Jewish community in Israel (1979), posters of the Israeli graphic designer Raphie Etgar (1990), and ephemera from American Jewish life (1976).

Specific events, movements, or individuals have often been the subject of a Judaica library exhibition. Among them were: Maimonides' Mishneh Torah (1979), Jewish thought in the sixteenth century (1980), Jewish thought in the seventeenth century (1982), Hasidism (1982), Christian Hebraism (1986), and the Dreyfus Affair (1984, 1994). In addition to the exhibition on Raphie Etgar, other exhibitions have featured the work of a single artist or designer: Shimon Sandhaus (1989), an Israeli graphic designer; David Moss (1989), an Israeli artist who prepared a Passover Haggadah; Ora Eitan (1990), an Israeli children's book illustrator; Avner Katz (1999), an Israeli artist and book illustrator; and Lionel Reiss (1997), an American Jewish artist.

Israel was frequently the subject of an exhibition. In addition to those of Israeli ephemera and Israeli art, there have been exhibitions on the relationship of the Jewish people to the Land of Israel (1973), the Israeli economy (1979), Israeli children's books (1981, 1992), resources for the study of Israel (1983), the Land of Israel (1985), the kibbutz (1987), Israeli memorial publications (1987), the Israeli theater (1989, 2004), archaeology in the Holy Land (1991), documenting Israel (1993), Jerusalem (1997), and Israeli popular music (1998).

On two occasions, the Division hosted traveling exhibitions. One was *Spiritual resistance: art from concentration camps 1940-1945*, from the Museum of Kibbutz Bet Lochamei HaGhettaot and sponsored by the Union of American Hebrew Congregations (1978). The other was *Jewish Art and Artifacts: Lost and Rediscovered: A Loan Exhibition from Poland*, sponsored by the Union of American Hebrew Congregations (1981). The Division also arranged an exhibition of Haggadot from the Harvard Judaica Collection at the B'nai B'rith Museum in Washington, D.C., in 1972. From time to time, the Division has loaned items to other institutions for inclusion in an exhibition, such as Israeli political posters to the Jimmy Carter Library in Atlanta, or a Judaica periodical to the United States Holocaust Memorial Museum.

Other programs utilized by the Judaica Division to bring the Judaica Collection to the attention of scholars and students have included lectures, symposia, and conferences. The lectures sponsored by the Judaica Division were often in conjunction with Judaica library exhibitions. Some focused on bibliographic topics such as Hebrew translations (1985), Hebrew manuscripts (1989, 1992), catalogs of Hebrew books (1995), and bindings of Hebrew books (1996). Others dealt with aspects of Jewish life in various countries: United States (1976, 1981, 1988), France (1972, 1984), Poland (1981, 1998), Russia (1980), Ukraine (1999), Hungary (1987), China (1992), and the Holocaust in Eastern Europe (1978). Yiddish culture was featured in several lectures (1979, 1980, 1985, 1986, 1987, 1990, 1995, 1996, 1997, 1999, 2002). Related to the Division's focus on documenting Israeli culture were lectures on different aspects of Israel: Israel-Diaspora relations (1973, 1982, 1984); film and television (1991, 1996); radio (2002); the ultra-orthodox religious sector (1979); archaeology (1991); theater (1989, 1991, 1995); popular music (1993); and memorial books (1987). Jewish and Israeli art was the topic of a number of lectures: Jewish ceremonial objects (1990); the American Jewish artist Lionel Reiss (1997); Israeli illustrators Ora Eitan (1990) and Avner Katz (1999); Israeli graphic designers Shimon Sandhaus (1989), Raphie Etgar (1990), and David Tartakover (1997); and Israeli artist David Moss (1989).

The Judaica Division has arranged conferences, colloquia, and symposia, many with national and international participation. Some have been devoted to Israel-related topics such as the study of Israel (1983, 1985), documenting Israel (1993), and the above-mentioned EVA conference (2002). Other programs called attention to new areas of collecting, such as Jewish and Israeli children's literature (1981, 1984), visual resources (Jewish films, 1989; Israeli films and other visual materials, 1997; Israeli film school productions, 1998), and Israeli political ephemera (1984); or to new initiatives in the Division's operations such as preservation (1981), cataloging (1988), and digitization (2002). Yet others aimed to highlight strengths in traditional areas of the Division's collecting efforts, such as the Jewish press (1985), Christian Hebraism (1986), Yiddish (1993), and the Dreyfus Affair (1994).

In addition, the Judaica Division cooperates with faculty departments and centers at Harvard in cosponsoring events or in arranging exhibitions in conjunction with their events. With the Center for Jewish Studies, the Division cosponsored lectures on Yiddish theater (1995), the Yiddish writer Leyzer Ran (1997), Jewish literature in Poland (1998 – with the Center for European Studies), and the Hebrew-Yiddish poet Abba Kovner (1999). The Division has arranged exhibitions in conjunction with Center programs on Jewish thought in the sixteenth century (1980), Jewish thought in the seventeenth century (1982), Hasidism (1982), Jewish Studies at Harvard (1988), Yiddish literature (1993), and the centennial of Zionism (1996).

Programs arranged in conjunction with the Semitic Museum included exhibitions on Jews in Germany (1982), Jews in Italy (1989), and Jewish ceremonial objects (1990), as well as a lecture on the Vatican's Hebrew manuscripts (1989). With the Center for European Studies the Division has cosponsored lectures on Jewish literature in Poland (1998) and radio in Israel (2002). With the Ukrainian Research Institute and the Slavic Division of Widener Library, the Division co-sponsored a lecture and video presentation on Jewish life in contemporary Ukraine (1999). Exhibitions were prepared on Jews in China in conjunction with a Fairbanks Center conference (1992), on Spanish Jewish studies in conjunction with a conference sponsored by the Department of Romance Languages and Literatures (1995), and on Jews in Latin America in conjunction with a Rockefeller Center Conference (1997).

The number of individuals who can attend a lecture, participate in a conference, or view an exhibition is limited, but publications—printed texts of lectures, published proceedings of conferences, and catalogs of exhibitions—bring the message of the events to a much wider audience. They also make the information permanently available as part of the literature in the field of Jewish Studies. The published catalogs of exhibitions of Israeli and American ephemera, for example, helped create an awareness in scholarly circles of the importance of these materials. Publication of the proceedings of the conference on documenting Israeli society called attention to the need for libraries to reexamine acquisition policies and to consider covering neglected types of Israeli publications. For this reason, the Judaica Division maintains an active program of publishing lectures, conference proceedings, and exhibition catalogs.

Also important in making Harvard's Judaica resources known to the scholarly community has been the participation of Judaica Division staff in meetings elsewhere of librarians and of scholars. Division staff have delivered papers at annual meetings of the Association of Jewish Libraries and the Association for Jewish Studies. In 1994, Division head Charles Berlin made a presentation on Harvard's Judaica Collection at the Fifth Congress of the European Association for Jewish Studies in Copenhagen. In 1996, he spoke about the Judaica Collection at the Israel Society of Special Libraries and Information Centers in Jerusalem and at Tel Aviv University; he also spoke about the collection at staff meetings at the Jewish National and University Library, the Tel Aviv Municipal Library, and the Diaspora Museum. In 1998, he spoke on the Judaica Collection at the Institut National des Langues et Civilisations Orientales in Clichy, the Alliance Israélite

Universelle in Paris, Jews' College in London, and the Oxford Center for Postgraduate Hebrew Studies. In 1999, he served on the Organizing Committee of the Conference on Judaica Archives in Europe for Archivists and Librarians—an initiative of the European Council of Jewish Communities—and at the conference in Potsdam he and Elizabeth Vernon, Judaica Technical Services Librarian in the Judaica Division, delivered papers. At the meeting of the International Federation of Library Associations (IFLA) in Jerusalem in 2000, he organized a panel, "Documenting Culture: The Case of Israel"—with the participation of Harvard, the Israel State Archives, and the Jewish National and University Library—and gave a paper on Harvard's "Documenting Israel" efforts. At the IFLA meeting in Boston in 2001, Elizabeth Vernon gave a paper on the Division's criteria for remote storage of Judaica. Also in 2001, Charles Berlin and Violet Gilboa made a presentation on archiving Israeli Internet websites at an invitational international conference on "Research in the Born-Digital Domain," sponsored by the Internet Archive and the National Science Foundation in San Francisco. Violet Gilboa's participation in the EVA conferences has been mentioned above.

Visits to the Harvard Judaica Collection by scholars, librarians, artists, writers, and Israeli government officials also serve to acquaint others with Harvard's Judaica resources. Each year brings visitors who come for a day or two, often longer, some to use the Judaica Collection, others just to visit Harvard. Of course, visiting professors or fellows at Harvard's Center for Jewish Studies stay for a semester or academic year, as do Wexner Israel Fellows at the Kennedy School of Government, and scholars at other Harvard departments and centers. When they return to their home institutions, be those in the United States, Israel, Europe, or elsewhere, they take with them information about Harvard's resources and the work of the Judaica Division. By the same token, travels by the Judaica Division staff, not only to such conferences as mentioned above but also on trips for collection development purposes, such as by Vernon to Europe, Gilboa to Israel, and Berlin to Israel and Europe—have also served to acquaint others with the Harvard Judaica Collection. All of this activity publicizes Harvard's Judaica resources in the scholarly community, fosters good relationships with individuals and institutions throughout the world, and often helps the Division to secure Judaica materials.

Reference assistance is also a means of furthering access to Harvard's Judaica holdings. Staff of the Judaica Division provide guidance to students preparing course research papers, senior honors theses, seminar papers, and dissertations, and Harvard faculty and visiting scholars frequently consult with Division staff. The Division offers orientation sessions on the Judaica Collection to groups as well as individuals. Division staff also provide instruction in the use of Judaica materials that offer new research opportunities. The Division prepares syllabi of Israeli films (in video) for the Hebrew-language courses at Harvard, and facilitates student access to many Israeli films via electronic reserve.

With an eye to encouraging student use of the Harvard Judaica Collection, the Division established in 1996 the *Harvard Judaica Collection Student Research Papers* series, which publishes outstanding honors theses or seminar papers that have utilized Harvard's Judaica library resources. In this way, the Division promotes awareness of the Judaica Collection, particularly of those materials that are unlikely to be found elsewhere, and in so doing also fosters innovative research projects. To date seven publications have appeared in this series: six honors theses and one book-length collection of undergraduate and graduate seminar papers on Jewish music. Some of the research papers relied on more traditional materials; others made use of special collections, such as Israeli and Jewish music.

Occasionally the Judaica Division has been featured in the media. Charles Berlin has spoken about the Judaica Collection on local television programs in Boston and Washington, D.C., and on a television program in Kiev, prerecorded at Harvard. Elizabeth Vernon spoke about the collection on a Paris radio program. Over the years, articles on the collection and on its exhibitions have appeared in Harvard publications—*Harvard Gazette*, *Harvard Magazine*, and *Harvard Library Bulletin*—and elsewhere, most recently an article in the magazine *Jerusalem Report* (April 30, 1998).

Thus, the Judaica Division's efforts to collect comprehensively have been accompanied by utilization of various means—cataloging, collection management, preservation, and a multi-faceted outreach program—to enhance access to the Harvard Judaica Collection in the service of scholarship.

Chapter Five

Securing the Resources for the Harvard Judaica Collection

THE ESSENTIAL COMPONENTS OF ANY EFFORT to build a great research collection in a university library include a favoring attitude on the part of the university and library administrations; dedication and vision of the librarians eager to develop such a collection; faculty interest in and commitment to the field of studies that the collection would support; availability of materials to be acquired; and the financial resources to support the effort.

In the case of Judaica, mention has been made of the positive reception accorded Judaica, particularly Hebraica, at Harvard from the earliest days of the College—an attitude reflected in modern times in the previously-quoted letter of November 23, 1929, from Professor Robert Blake to Lucius Littauer and, more recently, by President Derek Bok in 1976, when opening the campaign to establish a Center for Jewish Studies at Harvard:

> At Harvard, we have a special tradition to uphold in Jewish Studies—the tradition exemplified by the teaching and scholarship of the late Harry Wolfson, and the steady growth of books and other scholarly materials that have culminated in a Judaica Collection unequalled at an American university.
>
> With this tradition on which to build, we are determined to insure the continued vitality of teaching and research in this important field for generations to come.

The faculty component has also been present from the beginning—witness Harvard's earliest presidents who were Hebrew scholars and the establishment of the Hancock Professorship of Hebrew and Other Oriental Languages in 1764. In modern times seven endowed professorships in Jewish Studies have been established. In the Faculty of Arts and Sciences they are: Nathan Littauer Professorship of Jewish History and Philosophy (established in 1925), Harry Austryn Wolfson Professorship of Jewish

Studies (1975), Harry Starr Professorship of Classical and Modern Jewish and Hebrew Literature (1976), Jacob E. Safra Professorship of Jewish History and Sephardic Civilization (1978), Dorot Professorship of the Archaeology of Israel (1984), Martin Peretz Professorship of Yiddish Literature (1990). In the Divinity School there is the Albert A. List Professorship in Jewish Studies (1981). There are also three endowed visiting professorships in Jewish Studies: Gerard Weinstock Visiting Professorship of Jewish Studies (1976) and Nachshon Visiting Professorship of Modern Israel Studies (2001), in the Faculty of Arts and Sciences; and Caroline Zelaznik Gruss and Joseph S. Gruss Visiting Professorship in Talmudic Civil Law (1988) in the Law School. As for the role of librarians and the availability of materials, these elements have already been discussed above. Financial resources must now be considered, since they are such a key element.

In the course of the first half of the twentieth century, Harvard's Judaica Collection benefited greatly from the generosity of various donors, particularly Lucius Littauer and Lee Friedman. Their support included contributions for current use as well as gifts to establish Judaica endowments. This provided a substantial base that the Judaica Division has been able to enhance significantly thanks to the many generous alumni and friends of Harvard who have invested their time and money to assure that Harvard would have the financial resources needed to build and sustain its Judaica Collection.

Before establishment of the Judaica Division in 1962, Lucius Littauer had already done much for the future development of Judaica and Jewish Studies at Harvard. He endowed the first professorship in post-Biblical Jewish Studies at Harvard as well as the first Judaica book fund, and his series of gifts of collections of Hebraica laid the foundation for Harvard's Hebraica Collection. Similarly, Lee Friedman's generosity added Judaica and Hebraica collections, and also provided for the first time a permanent endowed Judaica librarian's position.

The Yiddish Collection, too, owes its establishment to gifts—those of Leo Wiener and Morris and James Loeb, as was noted in Chapter 2. Yiddish holdings were augmented beginning three decades later by the efforts of A. A. Roback in securing contributions from individuals for purchase of Yiddish books. The 1934 edition of the *Descriptive and Historical Notes* of the Harvard University Library, for example, mentions that among the donors to the Yiddish Collection were "Louis Bamberger and Felix Fuld, both of Newark, NJ, Louis Marshall of New York, Governor Herbert H. Lehman, of New York, Mr. and Mrs. Irving B. Mittel, of Dorchester, Mass."

Gifts for library processing were also made, notably by Lucius Littauer. In addition to his donations for the purchase of books or collections of books, Mr. Littauer, between 1930 and 1937, also supported the cataloging as well as the binding of the Hebraica that he gave to Harvard. These contributions were especially appreciated by the Library. Librarian of Harvard College Alfred C. Potter wrote to Mr. Littauer on March 14, 1930:

> I wish to assure you how highly I appreciate your thoughtfulness in thus providing for the arrangement and the cataloguing of the collection that you kindly gave us. When special collections are presented to the Library, the cataloguing of them often proves a great strain on our staff, which is barely large enough to carry on the regular routine work of the Library. I wish that all our benefactors realized this fact as you evidently do.

Seven years later, in his letter of September 27, 1937, Director of the Harvard University Library Keyes D. Metcalf was no less appreciative in responding to Mr. Littauer's additional contribution to complete the work on the Hebraica Collection:

> You may be assured the authorities here are gratified that to your magnificent gift of books you have so willingly added the indispensable costs of installation without which the books would lose much of their value. If all benefactors of the Library were as thoughtful, it would aid very considerably in our efforts to make available our collections.

After establishment of the Library's Judaica Division (then the Hebrew Division) in 1962, it soon became clear to the Division that development of the Judaica Collection into a world-class collection required additional funds. The generous contributions of donors in the first half of the twentieth century provided Harvard with a substantial Judaica Collection, and an initial endowment to sustain future growth of the collection. However, the continued development of the Judaica Collection would require additional funds on a regular, permanent basis and on a much larger scale. This meant securing substantial endowments for the Judaica Collection that would assure the availability of income each year—in perpetuity—for acquisitions, staffing, preservation, and other programs and activities that would enhance the Judaica Collection. The Division therefore committed itself to securing this financial support.

The first step was to establish the Friends of the Harvard Judaica Collection in 1970. Names of Harvard alumni were selected from the various Reunion Class Reports on the basis of autobiographical statements suggesting potential interest. Leonard Kaplan (Class of 1933, J.D. 1936), a Boston attorney, agreed in November 1970 to serve as president. In response to an invitation, several dozen alumni joined the new Friends group, which was to grow to several hundred members as a result of ongoing outreach. Leonard Kaplan was succeeded as president of the Friends of Judaica in March 1977 by William Lee Frost (Class of 1947, M.P.A. 1958), a New York attorney and president of The Lucius N. Littauer Foundation, who served through December 1996. Frost was succeeded by Jonathan M. Silver (Class of 1979), a Washington, D.C., venture capitalist, who served until December 2003. Silver was succeeded by David B. Keidan (Class of 1966, M.B.A. 1968), president of the New York investment firm The Buckingham Research Group, Inc.

The membership contribution was initially set at $25 per year (increased to $35 in 1992). The Judaica Division had a twofold goal. The first was to obtain additional funds for Judaica acquisitions. The second and strategically more important goal was to secure endowments for the Judaica Collection. The Friends of Judaica, it was hoped, would identify individuals who, after becoming acquainted with the Harvard Judaica Collection, would be interested in providing endowment funds. Friends of Judaica receive notices of Judaica library exhibitions, lectures, and other programs, as well as complimentary copies of many of the Library's Judaica publications, all of which keep Friends informed regarding developments in the Harvard Judaica Collection.

An indication of the potential benefit that endowments could bring to the Judaica Collection was already evident from the five Judaica endowments that had been established in the quarter century preceding the establishment of the Judaica Division. The Nathan Littauer Fund established by Lucius Littauer in 1937—the Library's first Judaica book fund endowment—was supplemented by an additional Judaica book fund endowment given by the Littauer Foundation in 1959. In addition, Judaica book funds were established by bequest of Max Davis (Class of 1922) in 1949, and in memory of Israel Matz by bequest of Sydney Matz (Class of 1921) in 1960. And, of course, there was the Lee M. Friedman endowment for Judaica, established by bequest of Mr. Friedman in 1957.

An opportunity to begin the implementation of this strategy presented itself in 1972. That year marked the eighty-fifth birthday of Harry Austryn Wolfson, the first incumbent of Harvard's Nathan Littauer Professorship of Jewish History and Philosophy and the first Honorary Curator of Judaica and Hebraica in the Harvard College Library. This was also the sixtieth anniversary of Professor Wolfson's graduation from Harvard in 1912. In appreciation of Professor Wolfson's role in the development of Harvard's Judaica Collection, the Judaica Division organized a campaign to establish

The Harry A. Wolfson Book Fund for Judaica in honor of these two milestones. With George H. Williams, Hollis Professor of Divinity at Harvard and a close friend of Wolfson, as chairman, the Division succeeded in meeting its goal of raising an endowment of some $85,000 from family, friends and former students of Professor Wolfson. This was celebrated at a gathering at the Library on November 2, 1972. The following year two additional Judaica book funds were established: The Alperin-Epstein Book Fund for Judaica, given by Jordan L. Alperin (Class of 1932) and his wife Esther T. Alperin (Class of 1934); and The Glory of Israel Hebrew Institute of East New York Book Fund for Judaica, established by the Institute at the time of its dissolution, in order to perpetuate the Institute's memory.

The success of the Judaica Division's initial fund-raising efforts demonstrated that there was potential support among alumni for Judaica and Jewish Studies at Harvard. In 1976, the University launched a campaign to raise funds to establish a Center for Jewish Studies at Harvard. The campaign, called The Program for the Harvard University Center for Jewish Studies, sought support for three major components: professorships, graduate student fellowships, and the Library's Judaica Collection. The Judaica Division had an active role in this campaign. The chairman of the campaign, Gerard Weinstock (Class of 1939, J.D. 1942), and the treasurer, William Lee Frost, were recruited from the Friends of the Harvard Judaica Collection, as were a number of members of the Program's National Committee. Campaign brochures were prepared by the University Development Office with much input from the Judaica Division. One of the brochures was devoted to the Judaica Collection and its need for more endowments and was widely distributed by the Judaica Division to the Friends of Judaica and other alumni. In the course of the campaign, the Division published three issues of a newsletter, *Harvard Judaica*, which contained news of the Judaica Collection and reports on the campaign's progress in securing Judaica book funds. In addition, the head of the Judaica Division participated in the Program's fundraising events in Boston, New York, Chicago, and Kansas City, and the Division provided potential donors to the Program with information about the need for Judaica library support.

The official launching of the Judaica library effort took place on May 3, 1976, in conjunction with the opening of the Judaica Division's American Bicentennial exhibition, "American Jewish Ephemera," introduced with a lecture by Professor Oscar Handlin. The brochure for the event listed 20 Judaica book funds, of which 12 represented new endowments established through the Program. One of them was The Joe and Emily Lowe Foundation Book Fund for Judaica for the acquisition, cataloging, and preservation of Judaica ephemera; the exhibition commemorated its establishment. In September 1977, the Judaica Division published *Harvard Judaica Bookplates: a Catalog of Bookplates Representing the Endowed Book Funds of the Harvard Judaica Collection.* The catalog, which included a facsimile of each fund's bookplate, listed 81 Judaica book funds; 73 of them had been established through the Program for the Harvard University Center for Jewish Studies. In October 1978, the Judaica Division issued a supplement listing 42 additional funds. By the conclusion of the campaign, the Judaica Division had succeeded in securing some 115 new Judaica endowments.

The Judaica Division continued to work to obtain new endowments. When the University launched a five-year fundraising effort in 1979, The Harvard Campaign, the Judaica Division participated by preparing and disseminating various brochures, plus a Judaica Bookplate Calendar, with information on the Judaica book fund as a campaign gift option. In 1986, in connection with the University's 350th anniversary celebration, the Judaica Division published a second edition of *Harvard Judaica Bookplates,* this time with 295 Judaica book funds. Through the years of The Harvard Campaign and subsequently to 1994, the number of Judaica book funds grew to 353. The new funds were listed in three supplements, appearing between 1989 and 1994.

From 1994 to 1999, Harvard conducted a university-wide fundraising effort—The University Campaign. Again the Judaica Division actively participated and prepared a number of Judaica fundraising publications that it widely disseminated. One such publication was the case statement, *Assuring the Future of the Harvard Judaica Collection through the University Campaign.* Also, a series of brochures presented the need for endowments for major aspects of the Judaica Collection: Israel, Jewish creative arts, Sephardica, Jewish press, Judaica digital library, and Judaica library student assistantships. Another series of brochures, issued annually from 1994 through 1998, listed Judaica book funds (with facsimiles of the bookplates) established by or in honor or in memory of members of the reunioning Harvard classes. Listings were indexed by fund, donor, honoree, and class. Through the years of The University Campaign and subsequently to 2001, the number of Judaica endowments grew to 410.

Early in 2002, the Harvard College Library announced that the minimum required to establish a book fund endowment would be increased on July 1, 2001, from $10,000 to $25,000. (The minimum had increased from $5,000 to $10,000 in 1990.) The Judaica Division disseminated this information to Judaica donors, Friends of Harvard Judaica, and others, and it invited those who might have been planning to establish a $10,000 Judaica book fund but had not yet done so to act before the July 1 deadline. This resulted in the establishment of 15 additional Judaica book funds. At present, the Library has 428 Judaica endowments, ranging from $5,000 to $1.5 million. (For a complete list of Judaica endowments, see Appendix E.)

Judaica book funds have proved to be an attractive option for donors. A book fund is a permanent named endowment fund, and only the annual income from the fund is used. A bookplate is designed and printed for each fund in consultation with the donor, and the bookplate is affixed to materials acquired from the fund's income. Each year the Judaica Division sends to the donor a report on acquisitions made possible by the fund. Many Judaica endowments continue to grow after their establishment, thanks to additional contributions over the years from the original donors, their family, and friends.

Judaica book funds have been established by Harvard College alumni from classes spanning over a century of Harvard's history, from Lucius Littauer of the Class of 1878 and Lee Friedman of the Class of 1893 to alumni who graduated in the 1990s. Many funds were also established by alumni of the various Harvard graduate schools, as well as by friends of Harvard. The bookplates printed for these funds reflect family histories: many were established in honor or in memory of parents or other family members, in some cases recording two or three generations of Harvard affiliations. Some book funds reflect a donor's interest in a particular aspect of Judaica and are restricted to, or express a preference for, areas such as Jewish music, Jewish art, Jewish theater, Jewish press, American Judaica, Eastern European Judaica, French Judaica, German Judaica, Latin American Judaica, Sephardic Judaica, Judeo-Arabic culture, Yiddish, Jewish history, Biblical studies, rabbinic literature, haggadot, Jewish philosophy, Jewish ethics, Hasidism, Reform Judaism, Jewish law, Jewish women, Jewish-Christian relations, medical Judaica, scientific Judaica, Jewish education, juvenile Judaica, bibliographic Judaica, Zionism, Israel, and Judaica ephemera. Some of the funds also provide support for Judaica library programs, such as lectures, exhibitions, and conferences. There are also endowments for Judaica library publications and for preservation of Judaica.

Endowments also support staff positions in the Judaica Division, the first of which was the Lee M. Friedman Bibliographer in Judaica, established through the bequest of Lee M. Friedman. The Lucius N. Littauer Foundation has provided endowments for other staff positions—the Littauer Hebraica Technical and Research Services Librarian and the Harvard National Judaica Librarians—as well as the Littauer Judaica Library Student Assistantships Endowment which provides the Division with funds to hire student assistants. Two other endowments also provide funds for student assistants: The Arthur L. Abrams Judaica Library Student Assistantship Endowment Fund and The Norman and Eleanor Rabb Judaica Library Student Assistantship Endowment Fund.

The Judaica Collection has also benefited from gifts from foundations and individuals for current use, just as it did from such gifts as those from Lucius Littauer in the 1930s and those secured by Lee Friedman two decades later. For example, grants from The Lucius N. Littauer Foundation supported the cataloging of Hebrew manuscripts and of Judeo-Arabic books; the acquisition of large collections of Judaica microfilms, sound recordings, and videotapes; and Judaica library conferences and publications. Grants from The Horace W. Goldsmith Foundation supported retrospective conversion of the Hebrew and Yiddish catalogs; and a grant from The S.H. and Helen R. Scheuer Family Foundation supported a conference on Jewish children's literature.

The generosity of donors to the Judaica Collection has enabled the Judaica Division to meet its goal of having Judaica acquisitions, staff positions, and library programs funded by income from its Judaica endowments. This is, of course, complemented by the very substantial support provided to the Judaica Collection by the Library in terms of infrastructure, technology, and the many services provided by the various units of the Harvard College Library and the Harvard University Library. The combination of Judaica endowments, together with the Judaica Collection's being an integral part of the Harvard College Library and Harvard University with their enormous intellectual and technical resources, produces the synergy that Professor Blake alluded to in his previously-quoted November 23, 1929, letter to Lucius Littauer: "The value of a collection such as this [Hebraica] is intrinsically greater when the collection is enshrined in one of the great libraries of this country, such as the Harvard Library is." The development of the Judaica Collection since that time, especially in the last four decades, attests to the accuracy of Professor Blake's statement. The support and encouragement of the Library and the University have had a multiplying effect on the efforts of the Judaica Division and have created an environment in which the Judaica Collection has flourished, and will continue to flourish, in its striving for the excellence that the Library and the University expect.

APPENDICES

Appendix A

Publications Related to the Harvard Judaica Collection

(Published by the Judaica Division of the Harvard College Library unless otherwise noted.)

Introductions to the Harvard Judaica Collection

The Judaica Collection at Harvard.
By Charles Berlin.
1971. [6] p.
Reprinted by the Judaica Division from *The Jewish Book Annual* (1968/69) on the occasion of the establishment of the Friends of the Harvard Judaica Collection.

An Introduction to the Harvard Judaica Collection.
(Guides to the Harvard Judaica Collection, no. 2)
1996. 24 p.

Hebrew Books in Harvard.
By Harry A. Wolfson.
1968. 12 p.
Reprinted by the Judaica Division from the *Harvard Alumni Bulletin* (April 29, 1932) on the occasion of the publication of the Harvard University Library's *Catalogue of Hebrew books.*

Hebrew Books in Harvard.
By Harry A. Wolfson.
1971. 12 p.
Reprinted by the Judaica Division from the *Harvard Alumni Bulletin* (April 29, 1932) on the occasion of the establishment of the Friends of the Harvard Judaica Collection.

The Yiddish Collection in the Harvard College Library
By A. A. Roback.
1929. [11] p.
Offprint from the *Harvard Alumni Bulletin* (April 25, 1929).

Documenting Israel.
(Guides to the Harvard Judaica Collection, no. 1)
1993. [12] p.

Bibliographic Catalogs

Catalogue of Hebrew Books.
Published by the Harvard University Library.
1968. 6 v.

Judaica.
Published by the Harvard University Library.
1971. 302 p. (Widener Library shelflist, vol. 39)

Index to Festschriften in Jewish Studies.
Compiled and edited by Charles Berlin.
Published by Harvard College Library and Ktav Publishing House (New York)
1971. xi, 319 p.

Catalogue of Hebrew Books: Supplement I.
Published by the Harvard University Library.
1972. 3 v.

Judaica in the Houghton Library.
Offprint from *Catalogue of Hebrew Books: Supplement I.*
1972. 193 p.

Hebrew Manuscripts in the Houghton Library of the Harvard College Library.
Prepared by Mordechai Glatzer; edited by Charles Berlin and Rodney Gove Dennis.
1975. 68 p.

Guide to Judaica Serials in Microform in the Harvard College Library.
1981. x, 32 p.

Guide to Judaica Microforms in the Harvard College Library.
1988. 8 p.

Guide to Judaica Videotapes in the Harvard College Library.
Prepared by Charles Berlin.
1989. 160, 80 p.

Yiddish Children's Books on Microfiche.
Prepared by Tammy Shemer.
1990. 246 p.

Catalog of the Bernice and Henry Tumen Collection of Jewish Ceremonial Objects in the Harvard College Library and the Harvard Semitic Museum.
Prepared by Violet Gilboa.
1992. 172 p.

Guide to Ladino Materials in the Harvard College Library.
Prepared by Aron Rodrigue.
1992. xii, 184, 60, 73 p.

Catalog of the Hebrew Collection at the Harvard College Library.
Edited by Charles Berlin.
Published by K. G. Saur (Munich)
1995. 11 v.

Hebrew Books from the Harvard College Library: Index to the Microfiche Collection.
Collection editor: Charles Berlin.
Published by K. G. Saur (Munich)
1996. x, 219 p.

Judaica Sound Recordings in the Harvard College Library: A Catalog.
Prepared by Violet Gilboa; edited by Charles Berlin.
1996. 3 v.

Local Press in Israel.
Prepared by Elizabeth Vernon.
1996. 41 p. (Guides to the Harvard Judaica Collection, no. 3)

Judaica Serials and Ephemera Microfilmed under The Strengthening Research Library Resources Program Title II-C of the Higher Education Act of 1965: Checklist Series

Checklist no. 1.
1979. vi, 78 p.

Checklist no. 1.
(2nd printing rev.).
1979. ix, 78 p.

Checklist no. 2.
1979. vii, 88 p.

Checklist no. 3: German Judaica Pamphlets.
1979. 74 p.

Checklist no. 4.
1980. xi, 81 p.

Checklist no. 5: French Judaica Pamphlets.
1980. 24 p.

Checklist no. 6.
1980. 46 p.

Checklist no. 7.
1980. ix, 50 p.

Checklist no. 8.
1981. xi, 76 p.

Checklist no. 9.
1982. 63 p.

Checklist no. 10: Slavic Judaica Pamphlets.
Prepared by the Library's Slavic Division.
1981. 107 p.

Checklist no. 11: Hebrew Pamphlets.
1983. (Microfiche.)

Checklist no. 12: English Pamphlets.
1984. (Microfiche.)

Checklist no. 13: Dutch Pamphlets.
1984. (Microfiche.)

Checklist no. 14: Spanish Pamphlets.
1985. (Microfiche.)

Checklist no. 15: Danish Pamphlets.
1985. (Microfiche.)

Checklist no. 16: Yiddish Pamphlets.
1988. (Microfiche.)

Exhibition Catalogs and Related Publications

The Jewish People and Palestine: A Bibliophilic Pilgrimage Through Five Centuries.
Lecture by Yosef Hayim Yerushalmi; catalog of the exhibition prepared by Charles Berlin.
1973. [238] p.

American Jewish Ephemera: A Bicentennial Exhibition from the Judaica Collection of the Harvard College Library.
Lecture by Oscar Handlin; catalog of the exhibition prepared by Charles Berlin.
1977. 7 p., 125 plates.

Knesset 9: An Exhibition of Ephemera from the 1977 Israeli Elections for the Ninth Knesset.
Prepared by Charles Berlin; foreword by Nadav Safran.
1978. [147] p.

German Judaica: A Sampling of Harvard's Library Resources for the Study of German Jewry.
Prepared by Stephen M. Poppel.
1982. 36 p.

Hasidism: The First Three Generations.
Prepared by Abraham Foxbruner.
1982. 16 p.

Contest of Symbols: The Sociology of Election Campaigns through Israeli Ephemera.
By Hanna Herzog; foreword by Sidney Verba.
1987. iv, 192 p.

Christian Hebraism: The Study of Jewish Culture by Christian Scholars in Medieval and Early Modern Times.
Symposium lectures: Krister Stendahl, Marc E. Saperstein, Aaron L. Katchen; exhibition and catalog prepared by Charles Berlin and Aaron L. Katchen, with text by Aaron L. Katchen.
1988. 58 p.

Past and Present in Hebrew Literary Translation.
Lecture and exhibition catalog by Gabriel Zoran.
1990. 40 p.
Reprinted by the Judaica Division from the *Harvard Library Bulletin* (Fall 1988).

Raphie Etgar: Posters.
Prepared by Raphie Etgar.
1990. [20] p.

China and the Jews: A Sampling of Harvard Library Resources for the Study of Jewish Life in China and Chinese-Jewish Relations.
Prepared by Irene Eber and Violet Gilboa.
1992. 52 p.

On Stage, Off Stage: Memories of a Lifetime in the Yiddish Theatre.
By Luba Kadison and Joseph Buloff with Irving Genn.
1992. 161 p.

The Founding of Harvard/Radcliffe Hillel: A Fiftieth Anniversary Exhibition.
Prepared by William Lee Frost.
1994. 11 p.

Zionism: A Centennial Exhibition.
Prepared by Charles Berlin.
1996. 16 p.

Latin America Judaica: A Sampling of Harvard Library Resources for the Study of Jewish Life in Latin America.
Prepared by Charles Berlin.
1997. 28 p.

The Range of Yiddish: Catalog of an Exhibition from the Yiddish Collection of the Harvard College Library.
Edited by Marion Aptroot and Charles Berlin with the assistance of Elizabeth Vernon; introductory essays: Marion Aptroot and Jeremy Dauber.
1999. iv, 72 p.

Catalog of an Exhibition of Paintings and Drawings by the Israeli Artist Avner Katz.
Edited by Charles Berlin and Violet Gilboa.
2002. 36 p.

Lectures

The Mind and Spirit of East European Jewry during the Holocaust.
By Erich Goldhagen.
1979. 18 p.

Realities and Dreams: Images of the World in Israeli Children's Literature.
By Bernard Dov Cooperman.
1983. 30 p.
Reprinted by the Judaica Division from the *Harvard Library Bulletin* (Spring 1983).

Israel and the Diaspora: Image and Self-image.
By Howard M. Sachar.
1984. 17 p.

Jewish Politics in East Central Europe Between the World Wars.
By Ezra Mendelsohn.
1984. 12 p.

The Dreyfus Affair.
By Paula Hyman.
1985. 9 p.

American Jewry or American Judaism.
By Nathan Glazer.
1988. 13 p.

Rewriting History in the Bible: The Book of Ruth vs. the Book of Chronicles.
By Meir Shalev.
1988. 13 p.

The New Christian Missionizing of the Thirteenth Century.
By Robert Chazan.
1988. 14 p.

Traditional Yiddish Literature: A Source for the Study of Women's Religious Lives.
By Chava Weissler.
1988. 24 p.

The Vatican Hebrew Manuscript Collection Against the Background of the History of the Vatican Library.
By Alfons Maria Cardinal Stickler.
1991. 9 p.

Constructive and Destructive Uses of Film as Propaganda: Case Studies from Jewish History.
By Marilyn Gold Koolik.
1992. 25 p.

Guides to the Perplexed in the Wilderness of Hebraica.
By Menahem Schmelzer.
1996. 23 p.

Popular Music in Israel: The First Fifty Years.
By Edwin Seroussi.
1996. 30 p.

Proceedings of Conferences

Jewish Children's Literature.
1985. vi, 74 p.

Jewish Leadership in Modern Times: A Symposium.
Jehuda Reinharz, Yizhar Smilanksy, and Yoram Peri.
1988. 25 p.

Judaica Librarianship: Facing the Future.
Edited by Charles Berlin.
1989. xii, 52 p.

Jewish Film and Jewish Studies.
Edited by Charles Berlin.
1991. 68 p.

What is Jewish in Jewish Literature?
Symposium: Aharon Appelfeld, Yoav Elstein; moderator: Sacvan Bercovitch.
1993. 27 p.

Documenting Israel.
Edited by Charles Berlin.
1995. xx, 238 p.

Electronic Imaging, the Visual Arts & Beyond: EVA 2002 Harvard Symposium Proceedings. Theme: U.S.-Europe-Israel Cooperation in 'Culture x Technology.'
Co-editors: Violet Gilboa and James Hemsley; produced by Val Duncan.
2003. [168] p.

Harvard Judaica Collection Student Research Papers Series

Sympathetic Portraits of Jews in Nineteenth-Century German Literature: The Cases of Wilhelm Raabe, Marie von Ebner-Eschenbach and Leopold von Sacher-Masoch.
By Adam J. Freudenheim.
1996. 40 p. (Student Research Papers, no. 1)

Musikah Mizrahit: From the Margins to the Mainstream.
By Eliezer Moshe Finegold.
1996. 41 p. (Student Research Papers, no. 2)

A Gilgul fun a Nigun: Jewish Musicians in New York, 1881-1945.
By Benjamin Loeffler.
1997. 63 p. (Student Research Papers, no. 3)

Cosmopolitan Critic: A Cultural Profile of Moshe Ibn Ezra.
By Samuel James Rascoff.
1998. 48 p. (Student Research Papers, no. 4)

Mi Yimalel—Who Will Retell?: Zionist Conceptions of Jewish History & the Ideal of the New Hebrew.
By Adam Jeremiah Levitin.
2000. v, 132 p. (Student Research Papers, no. 5)

Taking Up Their Harps on Foreign Soil: The Adaptations of the Arabic Desert Ode in Andalusian Poetry.
By Miriam Bayla Goldstein.
2000. iv, 56, [26] p. (Student Research Papers, no. 6)

Studies in Jewish Musical Traditions: Insights from the Harvard Collection of Judaica Sound Recordings.
Edited by Kay Kaufman Shelemay.
2001. xi, 222 p. (Student Research Papers, no. 7)

A Modern Aggadah: M.Y. Berdichevsky and the Reshaping of the Hebrew Narrative Tradition.
By Rachel Weinerman.
2004. (Student Research Papers, no. 8) (In preparation.)

Judaica Endowment Publications

Campaign Brochures

The Harvard University Library's Judaica Collection: The Program for the Harvard University Center for Jewish Studies.
Published by the University Development Office.
1976. 8 p.

Assuring the Future of the Harvard Judaica Collection through the University Campaign.
[1997]. 16 p.

Proposal to Establish an Endowment for the Israel Collection in the Harvard College Library.
1997. [12] p.

Proposal to Establish an Endowment for Israeli Business Publications in the Harvard College Library.
1997. [4] p.

Proposal to Establish an Endowment for Israeli Law Publications in the Harvard College Library.
1997. [4] p.

Proposal to Establish an Endowment for the Jewish Creative Arts in the Harvard College Library.
1997. [12] p.

Proposal to Establish an Endowment for the Jewish Press Collection in the Harvard College Library.
1997. [12] p.

Proposal to Establish an Endowment for the Judaica Digital Library in the Harvard College Library.
1997. [12] p.

Proposal to Establish an Endowment for Judaica Library Student Assistantships in the Harvard College Library.
1997. [8] p.

Proposal to Establish an Endowment for the Sephardic Collection in the Harvard College Library.
1997. [12] p.

Bookplate Catalogs

Harvard Judaica Bookplates: A Catalogue of Bookplates Representing the Endowed Book Funds of the Harvard Judaica Collection.
1977. 89 p.

Endowed Harvard Judaica Book Funds Established from September 1977 through October 1978.
1978. [5] p.
Supplement to *Harvard Judaica Bookplates* (1977).

Harvard Judaica Bookplate Calendar 1984.
1984. [26] p.

Harvard Judaica Bookplates: A Catalog of Bookplates Representing the Endowed Judaica Book Funds of the Harvard College Library.
1986. 80 p.

Judaica Book Funds in the Harvard College Library Established May 1986-September 1989.
1989. [8] p.
Supplement I to *Harvard Judaica Bookplates* (1986).

Judaica Book Funds in the Harvard College Library Established September 1989-September 1990.
1990. [9] p.
Supplement II to *Harvard Judaica Bookplates* (1986).

Judaica Book Funds in the Harvard College Library Established September 1990-December 1993.
1994. [15] p.
Supplement III to *Harvard Judaica Bookplates* (1986).

Judaica Book Funds in the Harvard College Library Established January 1994-December 1995.
1996. [15] p.
Supplement IV to *Harvard Judaica Bookplates* (1986).

Newsletters

Harvard Judaica, no. 1.
1980. 6 p.

Harvard Judaica, no. 2.
1981. 6 p.

Harvard Judaica, no. 3.
1982. 12 p.

Class Reunion Series

Judaica Book Funds Established by or through the Efforts of Members of the Class of 1954.
1994. [32] p.

Judaica Book Funds Established by or in Honor or Memory of Members of the Classes of 1915, 1920, 1925, 1930, 1935, 1940, 1945, 1950, 1955, 1960, 1965, 1975, 1980, 1985, 1990.
1995. [24] p.

Judaica Book Funds Established by or in Honor or Memory of Members of the Classes of 1916, 1921, 1926, 1931, 1936, 1941, 1946, 1951, 1956, 1961, 1966, 1971, 1976, 1981, 1986.
1996. [32] p.

Judaica Book Funds Established by or in Honor or Memory of Members of the Classes of 1912, 1927, 1932, 1937, 1942, 1947, 1952, 1957, 1962, 1967, 1972, 1977, 1982, 1987, 1992.
1997. [64] p.

Judaica Book Funds Established by or in Honor or Memory of Members of the Classes of 1878, 1893, 1913, 1918, 1923, 1928, 1933, 1938, 1943, 1948, 1953, 1958, 1963, 1968, 1973, 1978, 1983, 1988.
1998. [64] p.

Facsimile Editions

Print

Collected Writings of Rabbi Eliezer Charif.
1974. 363 p.
Issued on the occasion of the establishment of The Alperin-Epstein Book Fund for Judaica.

The Writings of Abraham Loeb Benjaminson.
Introduction by Yehuda Friedlander.
1994. xxvi, 370 p.
Issued on the occasion of the establishment of The Ruth and David A. Freedman Book Fund for Judaica.

Microform

Hebrew Books from the Harvard College Library.
Published by K. G. Saur (Munich) 1990.
4,934 titles on 11,453 microfiche.

Yiddish Books from the Harvard College Library.
Published by K.G. Saur (Munich) 2000.
2,603 titles on 5,229 microfiche.

Appendix B

Exhibitions Arranged by the Judaica Division of the Harvard College Library

(All materials exhibited were from the Harvard Judaica Collection, except for two visiting exhibitions, here marked with an asterisk.)

Hebrew Books at Harvard. 1968-1969

Passover Haggadahs. 1970

Passover Haggadahs. 1971

Jewish Portrait Studies by Lionel Reiss. 1971

Haggadahs from Harvard. 1972 (in Washington, D.C.)

Jewish Life in France. 1972

The Jewish Student Press in America. 1972

Wolfson of Harvard. 1972

The Jewish People & Palestine: A Bibliophilic Pilgrimage Through Five Centuries. 1973

American Jewish Ephemera. 1976

Around the World and Through the Years: Exhibition of Jewish Calendars. 1976

Passover Haggadot Acquired from 1972-1977. 1977

Israeli Posters Depicting Chess in Art. 1977

Jewish Calendars. 1977

Knesset 9 Election. 1977-1978

Jewish Berlin in the 1920s and 1930s. 1978

Thirty Years of Calendars from Israel. 1978

Harvard and Jewish Studies. 1978

Spiritual Resistance: Art from Concentration Camps 1940-1945. (Visiting Exhibition from the Museum of Kibbutz Bet Lochamei HaGhettaot.) 1978-1979 *

Purim 5739. 1979

Passover Haggadahs: Recent Acquisitions. 1979

Insulation and Involvement: Traditional Judaism in Modern Israel as Reflected in Religious Ephemera (Posters and Broadsides) from the Harvard Judaica Collection. 1979

The Israeli Economy as Reflected in Periodicals and Posters from the Harvard Judaica Collection. 1979

The Writings of Jacob Pat. 1979

Maimonides' Mishneh Torah: 800th Anniversary of a Book: Early Texts of the Mishneh Torah from the Harvard Judaica Collection. 1979

Jewish Thought in the 16th Century. 1980

Russian Judaica: A Sampling of Harvard's Resources for the Study of Russian Jewry. 1980

Children's Books from Israel. 1981

Judaica Preservation at Harvard. 1981

Jewish Art and Artifacts: Lost and Rediscovered: A Loan Exhibition from Poland. 1981 *

Jewish Thought in the 17th Century: A Selection of 17th-Century Publications from the Harvard Judaica Collection. 1982

German Judaica: A Sampling of Harvard's Library Resources for the Study of German Jewry. 1982

The Harvard Judaica Collection. 1982

High Holy Day Prayerbooks: A Selection of Prayerbooks from the Harvard Judaica Collection Exhibited on the Occasion of the Jewish New Year 5743. 1982

Hasidism: The First Three Generations. 1982

The Study of Israel: An Introduction to Harvard Library Resources for the Study of the State of Israel. 1983

Jewish Children's Literature. 1984

The Dreyfus Affair: A 90th Anniversary Exhibition from the Judaica Holdings of the Houghton Library. 1984

Contest of Symbols: The 1984 Elections in Israel as Reflected in Political Ephemera. 1984

The Jewish Press: An Introductory Exhibition. 1985

World Literature in Hebrew Translation. 1985

Jewish Music: An Introduction to Harvard Library Resources for the Study of Jewish Music. 1985

The Study of the Land of Israel. 1985-1986

Christian Hebraism: The Study of Jewish Culture by Christian Scholars in Medieval and Early Modern Times. 1986

Harvard Judaica Bookplates: Bookplates Representing Endowed Judaica Book Funds in The Harvard College Library. 1986

Utopia Between Dream and Reality: The Experience of the Israeli Kibbutz. 1987

Passover Haggadahs from the Harvard Judaica Collection: A Selection of Recent Acquisitions. 1987

Joseph Buloff's Two Worlds: Theatrical Memorabilia Illustrating a Master Artist's Sixty Years in the Yiddish and American Theaters. 1987

Jews of Hungary: An Introduction to the Library's Resources for the Study of Hungarian Jewry. 1987

The Twenty-Fifth Anniversary of the Library's Judaica Department: An Exhibition Celebrating Twenty-Five years of Library Progress in Jewish Studies at Harvard. 1987-1988

Israeli Memorial Publications: A Unique Approach to the Meaning of Death. 1987

Calendars From Israel. 1988

Passover Haggadahs from the Harvard Judaica Collection. 1988

Jewish Studies at Harvard: An Exhibition of Judaica Publications of Harvard Faculty, the Harvard University Press, the Harvard Judaica Collection, and Harvard Student Theses and Dissertations. 1988

Graphic Design in Israel: The Work of Shimon Sandhaus. 1989

A Song of David: The David Moss Haggadah. 1989

Italian Judaica: An Introduction to Harvard's Resources for the Study of Italian Jewry. 1989

The Israeli Theater: An Introduction to Harvard's Holdings Related to Theater in Israel. 1989

Illustrating Israeli Children's Literature: The Work of Ora Eitan. 1990

The Passover Haggadah in Memory of the Holocaust. 1990

Israeli Poster Art: The Work of Raphie Etgar. 1990

Jewish Ceremonial Objects from the Bernice and Henry Tumen Collection of the Harvard College Library and the Harvard Semitic Museum. 1990

A Century of Archaeology in the Holy Land. 1991

Passover Haggadot. 1991

Illustrated Calendars from Israel. 1991

The Hebrew Books from Harvard Microfiche Project. 1991

The Local Press in Israel Microfilm Project. 1991

New Periodicals from Israel. 1991

Children's Books from Israel. 1992

New Hebrew Literary Works From Israel. 1992

Passover Haggadot. 1992

China and the Jews. 1992

Ephemera from the 1992 Israeli Elections. 1992

Postage Stamps From Israel. 1992

Food in the Jewish Tradition. 1993

Documenting Israel. 1993

The Judaica Collection at 30: Thirty Years of Library Progress in Jewish Studies at Harvard. 1993

Yiddish Books at Harvard. 1993

The Founding of Harvard/Radcliffe Hillel: A Fiftieth Anniversary Exhibition. 1994

The Dreyfus Affair and the Self-Fashioning of Modern France: A Centennial Exhibition. 1994

Spanish-Jewish Studies: Present-Day Scholarship in Jewish Studies in Spain. 1995

Hebrew Bookbindings of the Eighteenth and Early Nineteenth Century: An Exhibition of the Physical Evidence Presented by Bookbinding and its Role in Interpreting the Place of the Book in Jewish Culture. 1996

Zionism: A Centennial Exhibition. 1996

Latin American Judaica. 1997

Jerusalem: A 3000 Year Anniversary Exhibition. 1997

The Works of Lionel Reiss. 1998

A Half-Century of Israeli Popular Music. 1998

The Work of Avner Katz. 1999

Preservation: Linking Source and Scholar: The Case of a Harvard Ketubah. 2000

Stars of the Yiddish Stage and Radio: The Careers of Seymour Rexite and Miriam Kressyn. 2002

Contemporary Israeli Theater Photographs: A Sampling of the Work of Gérard Allon, Gadi Dagon, and Eyal Landesman. 2004

Appendix C

Lectures Arranged by the Judaica Division of the Harvard College Library

Rare Hebrew Books and Manuscripts
Manfred Lehmann
1972

Reflections on the Jewish Historical Experience in France
Isadore Twersky
1972

The Jewish People and Palestine: A Bibliophilic Pilgrimage Through Five Centuries
Yosef H. Yerushalmi
1973

Jewish Daily Life in America Over the Past 100 Years
Oscar Handlin
1976

The Mind and Spirit of East European Jewry During the Holocaust
Erich Goldhagen
1978

Insulation and Involvement: Traditional Judaism in Modern Israel as Reflected in Religious Ephemera
Menachem Friedman
1979

The Labor Thread in the Fabric of Contemporary Jewish Life
Judah J. Shapiro
1979

Yiddish Dreams and American Reality: The Fate of a Culture
Joseph C. Landis
1980

Russian Jewry at the Beginning of the 20th Century
Richard Pipes
1980

The Jewish World of Israeli Youth
Simon N. Herman
1981

Realities and Dreams: Images of the World in Israeli Children's Literature
Bernard D. Cooperman
1981

American Jewry Today and Tomorrow: Reflections of a Historian
Oscar Handlin
1981

Jewish Life in Poland as Reflected in Jewish Literature
Arnold J. Band
1981

Israel and the Diaspora: The Interaction between the Israeli Labor Movement and the Jewish Labor Movement in Eastern Europe
Elkana Margalit
1982

The Legacy of German Jewry
Michael A. Meyer
1982

Jewish Politics in East Central Europe Between the World Wars
Ezra Mendelson
1984

Israel and the Diaspora: Image and Self-Image
Howard M. Sachar
1984

The Dreyfus Affair: Turning Point in Jewish History?
Paula Hyman
1984

Past and Present in Hebrew Literary Translation
Gabriel Zoran
1985

A Lifetime in the Jewish Musical Theater: Personal Reminiscences
Mike Burstyn
1985

Illustrations in Yiddish Books of the 16th and 17th Centuries: The Text, the Picture, and their Audience
Chone Shmeruk
1986

Traditional Yiddish Literature: A Source for the Study of Women's Religious Lives
Chava Weissler
1987

Christian Missionizing Among Jews in the Middle Ages: A Chapter in Jewish-Christian Relations
Robert Chazan
1987

Rewriting History in the Bible
Meir Shalev
1987

Observations on the Study of Hungarian Jewry
Michael Silber
1987

The Meaning of Death as Reflected in Israeli Memorial Publications
Alexander Barzel
1987

American Jewry or American Judaism?
Nathan Glazer
1988

New Approaches in Israeli Graphic Design
Shimon Sandhaus
1989

The Moss Haggadah: An Introduction
David Moss
1989

The Hebrew Manuscript Collections in the History of the Vatican Library
Alfons Maria Cardinal Stickler
1989

The Israeli Theater in the Last 10 Years
Noam Semel
1989

Illustrating Israeli Children's Literature
Ora Eitan
1990

Yiddish Culture in the Soviet Union
Michael Krutikov
1990

Poster Art in Israel
Raphie Etgar
1990

Jewish Ceremonial Objects as a Resource for Scholarship
Vivian Mann
1990

From Bible to Spade: Some Sidelights to History
Peter Machinist
1991

Constructive and Destructive Uses of Film Propaganda: Case Studies From Jewish History
Marilyn Koolik
1991

The Contemporary Israeli Theater
Hanna Marron
1991

Hebrew Medieval Manuscripts as Crosscultural Agents
Malachi Beit-Arié
1992

China and the Jews: Prospects for Research
Donald Leslie
1992

Popular Music in Israel
Edwin Seroussi
1993

To Be a Playwright in Israel
Yosef Bar-Yosef
1995

Guides to the Perplexed in the Wilderness of Hebraica: From Historical to Contemporary Bibliographies and Catalogs of Hebraica
Menachem Schmelzer
1995

Yiddish Theater *in* the Theater
Nahma Sandrow
1995

The Significance of Bindings in Interpreting the Place of the Book in Jewish Culture
Nicholas Pickwoad
1996

The New Age of Israeli Television
Nachman Shai
1996

Problems of American Yiddish Prose
Avraham Nowerstern
1996

Israeli Graphic Design
David Tartakover
1997

Documentation of Jewish Life as Reflected in the Works of Lionel Reiss, American Jewish Artist
Tom L. Freudenheim
1997

Leyzer Ran and his Place in Yiddish Literature
Marcus Moseley
1997

The Polish Jewish Writer After World War Two
Monika Adamczyk-Garbowska
1998

The Work of Avner Katz: Israeli Author and Book Illustrator
Avner Katz
1999

Jewish Life in Contemporary Ukraine through the Eyes of a Television Camera
Simon Burd
1999

Turning a Hebrew Kibbutz into a Yiddish Shtetl: Abba Kovner's Attempt to "Judaize" Zionism
Dina Porat
1999

Radio and Nationalization: From the BBC to the "Voice of Israel"
Derek Penslar
2002

Stars of the Yiddish Stage and Radio: The Careers of Seymour Rexite and Miriam Kressyn
Caraid O'Brien
2002

Appendix D

Conferences, Symposia, and Colloquia Arranged by the Judaica Division of the Harvard College Library

Children's Books From Israel. (Symposium) 1981

International Preservation Microfilming Conference. 1981

The Study of Israel: A Symposium. 1983

Jewish Children's Literature. (Conference) 1984

Political Culture—What Does Election Propaganda Material Teach Us? (Symposium) 1984

The Jewish Press. (Conference) 1985

In Search of Identity: The Study of the Land of Israel in the 19th and 20th Centuries. (Symposium) 1985

Christian Hebraism. (Colloquium) 1986

Jewish Leadership in Modern Times. (Symposium) 1987

Judaica Librarianship: Facing the Future. (Conference) 1988

Jewish Film and Jewish Studies. (Conference) 1989

What is Jewish in Jewish Literature? (Symposium) 1992

Documenting Israel. (Conference) 1993

The Range of Yiddish. (Symposium) 1993

The Dreyfus Affair. (Symposium) 1994

Visual Media as the Documentation of Israeli Culture. (Symposium) 1997

The Role of Israeli Film School Productions in Israeli Cinematography. (Symposium) 1998

EVA Harvard Symposium: US—Europe—Israel Cooperation in 'Culture *x* Technology.' 2002

Appendix E

Judaica Endowments in the Harvard College Library

17th Century Judaica Book Fund
Established by The Lucius N. Littauer Foundation

18th Century Judaica Book Fund
Established by The Lucius N. Littauer Foundation

19th Century Judaica Book Fund
Established by The Lucius N. Littauer Foundation

20th Century Judaica Book Fund
Established by The Lucius N. Littauer Foundation

21st Century Judaica Book Fund
Established by The Lucius N. Littauer Foundation

The Arthur L. Abrams Judaica Library Student Assistantship Endowment Fund
Established by Susan L. and Alan V. Abrams, '63

Robert T. Abrams Judaica Book Fund
Established by Betsy Friedman Abrams, William Friedman Abrams, David Jacob Abrams, '85, Joel Henry Abrams, '90

Abramson Family Book Fund for Judaica
Established by Edward M. Abramson, '57, LL.B. '60

Harry A. Abramson Memorial Book Fund
Established by Edith and Harold Abramson, and their children Andrew, Richard, Lawrence, Anne

Clifford R. Adler Judaica Book Fund
Established by Clifford R. Adler, '77

George G. Adler Book Fund for Judaica
Established by James B. Adler, '53 and Esthy Adler

Mollie Barron Adler Book Fund for Judaica
Established by James B. Adler, '53 and Esthy Adler

Lassor and Fanny Agoos Book Fund for Judaica
Established by The Lassor and Fanny Agoos Charity Fund

Michael and Betsy Alderman Judaica Book Fund
Established by Michael Alderman, '58

Alperin-Epstein Book Fund for Judaica
Established by Jordan L. Alperin, '32 and Esther T. Alperin, '34

Wesley S. and Grace K. Alpert Book Fund for Judaica
Established by Grace K. and Wesley S. Alpert, '47

Dr. & Mrs. S. Y. Andelman Judaica Book Fund
Established by S. Yale Andelman, '35

William H. Angoff Class of 1940 Judaica Book Fund
Established by his wife Eleanor Wolk Angoff, and his children Carolyn J. Angoff, Douglas M. and Robin G. Angoff

Stuart and Phyllis Applebaum Family Judaica Book Fund
Established by Stuart A. Applebaum, '57

Aserkoff Family Judaica Book Fund
Established by Ralph D. Askeroff, '58 and Jean Askeroff

Avner Ash and Rosemary Reiss Book Fund for Judaica
Established by Avner D. Ash, '71 and Rosemary Reiss, '76

Charles Auerbach Judaica Book Fund
Established by David L. Auerbach, '57, LL.B. '55, Susan Auerbach and their children Deborah Auerbach Reisner and Jonathan S. Auerbach

Isaac and Carol Auerbach Book Fund for Judaica
Established by Isaac L. Auerbach

Benjamin and Alice Banks Book Fund for Judaica
Established by Benjamin M. Banks, '26, M.D. '30

Leonard Baron Judaica Book Fund
Established by his father Harry Baron and his brothers Robert B. Baron, Richard I. Baron

Jacob Louis Barowsky Book Fund for Judaica
Established by Adeline Seamon Barowksy, family and friends

Barron Family Book Fund for Judaica
Established by Carl F. Barron, Ruth L. Barron and their children Diane, Marilyn, Kenneth

Barrow Family Book Fund for Judaica
Established by Stephen Y. Barrow, '58

Benson L. Baskin Judaica Book Fund
Established by Martin S. Baskin, '54 and Susan Baskin Bernhard

Meyer A. Baskin Judaica Book Fund
Established by his children Jonathan Noel Baskin, '61, Kathy Baskin Davidson, Marc Nathaniel Baskin, '73, his sister Ruth Baskin White and his brother Leonard D. Baskin, '50

Samuel Jacob Beck Judaica Book Fund
Established by Anne G. Beck

Louis and Leah Beiner Book Fund for East European Judaica
Established by the Citrin family

The Daniel J. Beller Judaica Library Fund
Established by Daniel J. Beller, '68

Harry and Ruth Benet Book Fund for Judaica
Established by Mr. and Mrs. Harry Benet

Benson Book Fund for Judaica
Established by B. Robert Benson, '43 and Richard L. Benson, '48

Berlin Family Judaica Book Fund
Established by Charles Berlin, '58, Ph.D. '63 and Judith Armet Berlin and their children Anne D. Berlin, '87, J.D. '90 and Jonathan M. Berlin, '92

Charles Berlin Book Fund for Bibliographic Judaica
Established by The Max Richter Foundation

Charles Berlin Thirtieth Anniversary Judaica Book Fund
Established by The Lucius N. Littauer Foundation and William Lee Frost, '47, M.P.A. '58

Berman Family Judaica Book Fund in memory of Edith and Samuel Berman
Established by their children Ida, Mary, Isaac ,'29, Morris, Ernest, Edward, Gertrude, Helen, Esther, Leona

Berman Judaica Book Fund in memory of Goldie Cohen Berman
Established by Isaac Berman, '29, Robert A. Berman, and Stephen S. Berman

Madeleine and Mandell Berman Judaica Book Fund
Established by Mandell L. Berman, '40

Dr. Saul Berman Class of 1916 Judaica Book Fund
Established by Edith G. Weisbuch and Manuel Weisbuch, '23

Harold and Rosalind Bernstein Judaica Book Fund
Established by Harold Richard Bernstein, '39

Esther Alix Bilski Memorial Book Fund for Judaica
Established by Berthold Bilski

Herbert and Evelyn Birnbaum Book Fund for Judaica
Established by Herbert Birnbaum, '47

Jennie and Samuel Birnbaum Judaica Book Fund
Established by Herbert Birnbaum, '47, Eugene Birnbaum, Ira Birnbaum, Gerald Birnbaum

Nathan and Robin Birnbaum Book Fund for Judaica
Established by Nathan S. Birnbaum, '68

Dr. Haim Blanc Memorial Book Fund
Established by William Lee Frost, '47, M.P.A. '58

Samuel H. and Arlene Zelda Bloom Judaica Book Fund
Established by Samuel H. Bloom, '39

Bloom-Kaplan Judaica Book Fund
Established by Edward C. Bloom, '52, J.D. '55

Max J. Blum Book Fund for Judaica
Established by Elaine and Melvin Merians

Philip S. Blumberg Judaica Book Fund
Established by Joan Blumberg Booth, Edgar H. Booth, J.D. '53 and S.M. Louis Fund, Inc.

Joyce & Michael Bohnen Book Fund for Judaica
Established by Michael J. Bohnen, '68, J.D. '72

Chaya Bookstein Book Fund for Judaica
Established by Haim H. Chiswik, '37

The Boruchoff Family Judaica Book Fund
Established by S. Arthur Boruchoff, '45, Anna Silverman Boruchoff, Susan E. Boruchoff, '77, David Alan Boruchoff, '80, M.A. '81, Ph.D. '88 and Judith Boruchoff

Brachman-Yenkin Family Judaica Book Fund
Established by Merom, '58 and Judith Brachman, '60 and Bernard K. Yenkin, M.B.A. '54

Esther M. and Beryl D. Brem Judaica Book Fund
Established by Jacob Brem, '27, M.D. '31

Brenner Family Judaica Book Fund
Established by Joseph Brenner and family

Elizabeth and Harry Brodie Judaica Book Fund
Established by Mandell L. Berman, '40

Howard Scott Bronstein Book Fund for Judaica
Established by The Eugene and Estelle Ferkauf Foundation

Lauren Robin Bronstein Book Fund for Judaica
Established by The Eugene and Estelle Ferkauf Foundation

Ronald Seth Bronstein Book Fund for Judaica
Established by The Eugene and Estelle Ferkauf Foundation

Bronstein-Bronson Judaica Book Fund
Established by family and friends

Judge and Mrs. Matthew Brown Judaica Book Fund
Established by Matthew Brown, LL.B. '29

Florence and Samuel Brownstein Judaica Book Fund
Established by Martin H. Brownstein, '56

Daniel and Florence Burnstine Book Fund for Judaica
Established by Richard C. Burnstine, '50, M.D. '54

Leone and Merle J. Bushkin Judaica Book Fund for Jewish Children's Literature
Established by Merle J. Bushkin, '56, M.B.A. '60 and Leone Bushkin, Ed.M. '58

Canner Judaica Book Fund
Established by Arnold H. Canner, '28, Betty J. Canner, Carol Canner, M.A. '60 and Carl Canner, '61

Eliot D. and Blanche G. Canter and Family Judaica Book Fund
Established by Eliot D. Canter, BSCE '35

James J. Canter and Ida Canter Judaica Book Fund
Established by Martin D. Schwartz, '38

Caro Book Fund for Judaica
Established by The Wilma V. Birkhoff Trust

Leo & Esther Charnes Judaica Book Fund
Established by Frank Denny

Samuel and Rachel Chiswik Book Fund for Judaica
Established by Haim H. Chiswik, '37

Barney and Celia Citrin Book Fund for East European Judaica
Established by the Citrin family

Joel L. and Rhoda E. Clarke Judaica Book Fund
Established by Joel L. Clarke, '40

The Class of 1959 Judaica Book Fund
Established by members of the Class of 1959

Amy and Saul Z. Cohen Book Fund for Juvenile Judaica
Established by Saul Z. Cohen, LL.B. '52

Benjamin W. and Mildred A. Cohen Judaica Book Fund
Established by their sons, Richard L. Cohen, '45, Herbert M. Cohen, '46, Howard I. Cohen and their families

Eli and Bessie Cohen Judaica Book Fund
Established by Deborah and Zvi Cohen, '53 and their children Michael, '82, James, '83, and Eric, '87

Martin E. and Alice W. Cohen Book Fund for Judaica
Established by Martin E. Cohen, '36

Richard L. Cohen Judaica Book Fund
Established by his wife and daughters, Frances, Miriam and Judith

Rosalie Palter Cohen and Joseph Cohen, M.D. Family Book Fund for Judaica
Established by Carmel Jonathan Cohen, '54, Babbette Goodman Cohen, Lisa G. Cohen, M.A. '85, Jonathan G. Cohen

Judaica Book Fund
Established by the bequest of Steven James Cohen, '57, LL.B. '60

Cohn Judaica Book Fund
Established by Bertram J. Cohn, '47, Theodore Cohn, '44, William Lee Frost, '47, M.P.A. '58 and Henry R. Liss, '46

Edward M. Cowett 1951 Memorial Judaica Preservation Fund
Established by Wilbur A. Cowett, '45

Frank and Harriet Croman Memorial Judaica Book Fund
Established by Edward L. Croman, '60

Abraham Danciger Judaica Book Fund
Established by David K. Danciger, '46

Stuart J. and Joan B. Danoff Judaica Book Fund
Established by Stuart J. Danoff, '52, Joan B. Danoff, Nancy L. Danoff, '79, Susan A. Danoff and William A. Danoff, '82

Jacob Davis Judaica Book Fund
Established by Jacob Davis, '19

Joseph M. Davis Book Fund for Judaica
Established by Joseph M. Davis, Jr., '32

Max Davis Book Fund for Judaica
Established by bequest of Max Davis, '22

Mark Jared Davlin Judaica Book Fund
Established by Irwin H. Davlin, '48

Ephraim Deinard Memorial Judaica Book Fund
Established by Amos S. Deinard, '57 and Miriam J. Kelen

Delfiner-Sperber Book Fund for Judaica
Established by Abraham D. Sperber, '21, M.B.A. '23 and Charlotte Sperber

Paul and Mary Dessauer Judaica Book Fund
Established by Paul, '26 and Mary Dessauer

The Alan Doft Judaica Book Fund
Established by Alan, '54 and Elisabeth Doft

Alan ('54) and Elisabeth Hoffman Doft Book Fund for Judaica
Established by Alan, '54 and Elisabeth Doft

The Benjamin J. Doft Judaica Book Fund
Established by Alan Doft, '54

The Michael, Jonathan and Rachel '95 Doft Judaica Book Fund
Established by Alan, '54 and Elisabeth Doft

The Pauline and Emanuel Doft Judaica Book Fund
Established by Alan, '54 and Elisabeth Doft, Michael, Jonathan and Rachel '95 Doft

Druker Family Judaica Book Fund
Established by Joyce T. and Isaac E. Druker, '58

Gloria King Elkin, A.B. 1942 Book Fund for Judaica
Established by Milton Elkin, '37, M.D. '41

Emet Book Fund for Judaica
Established by Serene P. Shanus, '77 and Phillip H. Feuer, '77 and their children Rose R.S. Feuer and Abigail E.S. Feuer

Eve and Harry Englander Book Fund for Judaica
Established by Thelma and Ray Goldberg, '48 and their children Marc, Jennifer, Jeffrey

Epstein Family Book Fund for Judaica
Established by Maury Epstein, '32, LL.B. '35 and Leo Epstein, '37

Hyman Epstein Book Fund for Judaica
Established by Melvin, '59 and Rachel S. Epstein

Jacob and Frieda Epstein Book Fund for Judaica
Established by Charles Joseph Epstein, '55, M.D. '59 and Lois Barth Epstein, '55, M.D. '59

The Sonia Furman Epstein Judaica Book Fund
Established by David Epstein, '57, J.D. '60

Feldstein Fund for Judaica
Established by Vivian C. Feldstein

Fialkow Family Judaica Book Fund
Established by Jay L. Fialkow, '48 and Jane M. Fialkow

The Nathan L. and Bertha Offenbach Fineberg Judaica Book Fund
Established by Bertha Offenbach Fineberg, '31

Fischman Family Judaica Book Fund
Established by William J. Fischman, '43

Fishman Family Book Fund for Judaica
Established by Susan R. Fishman and Lawrence M. Fishman, '55, M.D. '60 and their children Robin L. and Matthew E. Fishman, '80, Charles N. Fishman, '83, Betsy R. Fishman, '88, Andrew K. Fishman

Herbert Israel Fishman Judaica Book Fund
Established by bequest of Herbert Israel Fishman, '55

Fleisher Family Judaica Book Fund
Established by Lillian G. Fleisher, Michael H. Fleisher and Peter J. Fleisher

Folkman Judaica Book Fund
Established by David, '57 and Susan Folkman

Frackman Family Book Fund for Judaica
Established by Andrew J. Frackman, '77 and Emily Braun

Fraiman Family Judaica Book Fund
Established by Melvin Fraiman, '46, Beatrice Fraiman and their children Richard, Douglas, Phillip, '78

Nathan and Bessie Franklin Judaica Book Fund
Established by Herbert M. Franklin, '55 and Barbara B. Franklin

Hirsh and Rosalind Freed Book Fund for Judaica
Established by Hirsch Freed, '30, LL.B. '36

Morton and Alice Freedland Judaica Book Fund
Established by Morton Freedland, '37

Ruth & David A. Freedman Book Fund for Judaica
Established by Stanley A. Freedman, '43, Albert L. Freedman, '46 and Barbara A. Wolfson

French Jewish Book Fund for Judaica
Established by Thomas B. Lemann, '49, LL.B. '52

Friedberg Fund for Medical & Scientific Judaica
Established by Lillian Adlow Friedberg, '18, A.M. '19, Judith E. Friedberg, '42, Simeon A. Friedberg, '46 and Aaron L. Friedberg, '78

Friedberg Judaica Book Fund
Established by Judith E. Friedberg, '42, Joan B. and Simeon A. Friedberg, '46, Aaron L. Friedberg, '78, Ph.D. '86, Susan Friedberg Kalson, '80 and Betsy Friedberg

Rose and Nathan Friedlander Judaica Book Fund
Established by Ruth and Richard Rosenbloom, '54, M.B.A. '56

Alfred and Esther Friedman Book Fund for Judaica
Established by their children Jack, M.B.A. '69, Frank, Stanley, Melvin

Bennett Friedman Judaica Book Fund
Established by K. Bruce Friedman, '50

Lee M. Friedman Bequest
Established by bequest of Lee M. Friedman, Class of 1893

William S. Friedman Judaica Book Fund
Established by Nathan J. Friedman and family

William Stix Friedman Judaica Book Fund
Established by Helene Schmitz Friedman

Robert Frost Book Fund for Judaica
Established by Eva Frost, Richard H. Frost, Theodore Frost, William Lee Frost, '47, M.P.A. '58 and Judith Frost Levine, '51

William Lee Frost Judaica Book Fund
Established by Bertram J. Cohn, '47

Michael A. and Leslie B. Gaffin Judaica Book Fund
Established by Leslie B. and Michael A. Gaffin, '65

Ganick Family Judaica Book Fund
Established by Saul S. Ganick, '30

Paul William and Philip C. Garber Judaica Book Fund
Established by Paul William Garber, '56, J.D. '61 and Philip C. Garber, '56, J.D. '61

Rubin E. Garber and Sarah R. Garber Judaica Book Fund
Established by Paul William Garber, '56, J.D. '61 and Philip C. Garber, '56, J.D. '61

Ruth Guttfreund Gardner Judaica Book Fund
Established by Arnold B. Gardner, LL.B. '53

Getz Judaica Book Fund
Established by Joel Ari Getz, '86

Gilfix Family Judaica Book Fund
Established by Matthew E. Gilfix, '58, M.B.A. '61

Gindi Associates Book Fund for Judaica
Established by The Gindi Associates Foundation, Inc.

William M. and Rae M. Ginsburg Judaica Book Fund
Established by William M. Ginsburg, '37

Belle M. and Samuel H. Glaser Book Fund for Judaica
Established by Samuel H. Glaser, '28

Glazier Family Judaica Book Fund
Established by Henry S. Glazier, '31

Glory of Israel Hebrew Institute of East New York Book Fund for Judaica
Established by the Glory of Israel Hebrew Institute of East New York

Ethel C. and William H. Gofen Book Fund for Judaica
Established by William H. Gofen, M.B.A. '54

William and Cindy Gold Judaica Book Fund
Established by William Gold, '49

Anne and Max Goldberg Book Fund for Judaica
Established by Thelma and Ray A. Goldberg, '48 and their children Marc, Jennifer, Jeffrey

Janet K. and Dr. Max J. Goldberg
Established by George A. Goldberg, '63, M.D. '68

Joseph and Rose Goldberg Memorial Judaica Book Fund
Established by David A. Goldberg, '54, J.D. '57

Marjorie and Edward Goldberger Book Fund for Judaica
Established by Edward Goldberger, LL.B. '31

Agnes W. Goldman Judaica Book Fund
Established by Robert I. Goldman, '54

Dr. Joseph and Clara Z. G. Goldman Judaica Book Fund
Established by Dorothy Goldman Sparrow, Ph.D. '65 and Marvin Sparrow, LL.B. '50

Goldman-Levy Book Fund for Judaica
Established by Allan B. Goldman, '58, LL.B. '63 and Eleanor Levy Goldman

Sidney and Harold Reich Goldmann Book Fund for Judaica
Established by Harold Goldmann, '39 and Sidney Goldmann, '24

Goldstein Judaica Book Fund
Established by Robert V. Goldstein, '59 and Nancy B. Goldstein

Goldweitz Family Book Fund for Judaica
Established by Mark R. Goldweitz, '67

Golombeck Family Judaica Book Fund
Established by Alfred Miller, '48, LL.B. '51

The Rabbi Abram V. Goodman Memorial Judaica Book Fund
Established by bequest of Abram V. Goodman, '24

Sophia S. and Alexander S. Goodman Judaica Book Fund
Established by Estate of Sophia S. Goodman

Solomon Joseph Gootman Judaica Book Fund
Established by Gerald M. Gootman, '59, M.B.A. '64 and Elliot C. Gootman, '65

Morris J. Gordon Judaica Book Fund
Established by Marvin A. Gordon, '58

Marion and Harold Green Book Fund for Judaica
Established by Richard M. Rosenberg, '56 and Donna Green Rosenberg and their children David, Deborah and Miriam

Allan J. Greenberg '28 Judaica Book Fund
Established by Janis Van C. Greenberg and Eldon Van C. Greenberg, '65

Arnold C. Greenberg Book Fund for Judaica
Established by Arnold C. Greenberg, '55, LL.B. '58

The Greyser Family Judaica Book Fund (A)
Established by Stephen A. Greyser, '56, M.B.A. '58, D.B.A. '65

The Greyser Family Judaica Book Fund (B)
Established by Stephen A. Greyser, '56, M.B.A. '58, D.B.A. '65

Greyser Family Judaica Book Fund for Jewish Music
Established by Stephen A. Greyser, '56, M.B.A. '58, D.B.A. '65

Morris Greyser Book Fund for Judaica
Established by Stephen A. Greyser, '56, M.B.A. '58, D.B.A. '65

P. Irving Grinberg Judaica Book Fund
Established by Carol G. Lederer, Marion G. Preston, and Paul I. Grinberg, Jr. '41, M.B.A. '43

Pat and Eleanor Groper Book Fund for Judaica
Established by Earle Pat Groper, '54

Casper M. Grosberg Judaica Book Fund
Established by The Grosberg Family Charity Fund

The Gross-Spertus Fund for Books About Jewish Art
Established by William L., '61 and Lisa Spertus Gross, Daniella Gross-Barkay and Adi Barkay, Aaron Gross, Noah and Avital Gross

Joseph B. and Esther L. Grossman Book Fund for Judaica
Established by Bernard D. Grossman, '39, Everett L. Grossman, '48 and Pearl H. Goldberg

Max and Corinne Grossman Book Fund for Judaica
Established by Gloria and Frederick M. Grossman, '57 and their children Adam, Brian, Sara and Eric

Samuel Grossman Judaica Book Fund
Established by Allen Grossman, LL.B. '51

Leon I. and Louise S. Gubin Judaica Book Fund
Established by Leon I. Gubin, '29, J.D. '32

Abraham S. and Irene Guterman Book Fund for Judaica
Established by Abraham S. Guterman, J.D. '36

Beatrice Z. and Harry A. Harris Judaica Book Fund
Established by Katherine M. (Safford) '47, Ph.D. '54 and George Harris, '49, LL.B. '52

Harvey A. Harris Judaica Book Fund
Established by Harvey A. Harris, '58, J.D. '61

Leo Hartfield Book Fund for Judaica
Established by Hartfield-Zodys, Inc.

Max Hartfield Book Fund for Judaica
Established by Preston J., '32 and Gertrude Kline

Harvard-Littauer Judaica Endowment
Established by The Lucius N. Littauer Foundation

Harvard National Judaica Librarians Endowment
Established by The Lucius N. Littauer Foundation

Hertzberg Family Judaica Book Fund
Established by David Hertzberg, '63, Joseph Hertzberg, '64, Daniel Hertzberg

Abraham Hertzberg Judaica Book Fund
Established by Joan N. Hertzberg

Sigmund and Estel Herzstein Judaica Book Fund
Established by Robert E. Herzstein, '52

George H. and Edythe F. Heyman Book Fund for Judaica
Established by William H. Heyman, J.D.'73 and John A. and Lesley S. Heyman and Mallory and Brett

Jennie and Simon Hill Judaica Book Fund
Established by Louis L. Hill, '24

Anne & Benjamin Hinerfeld Book Fund for Judaica
Established by Ruth and Norman Hinerfeld, '51, M.B.A. '53

Edna R. and Maurice J. Hoffman '27 Book Fund for Judaica
Established by Alan, '54 and Elisabeth Doft, Michael, Jonathan and Rachel, '95 Doft

Michael and Ida Hoffman Family Book Fund for Judaica
Established by Maurice J. Hoffman, '27 and Alan Doft, '54

Robert D. Hoffman Book Fund for Judaica
Established by Chippe Adlow Hoffman, '24

Goldie Holleb Judaica Book Fund
Established by Betsy and Jack L. Karp, LL.B. '62

Dr. Albert C. Holzman, D.M.D. Class of 1911 Book Fund for Judaica
Established by Betty and J. William Pinkos, '38

Louis A. Horvitz Judaica Book Fund
Established by Louis A. Horvitz, '29

Horwitz and Band Family Judaica Book Fund
Established by Susan Band Horwitz and Marshal S. Horwitz, '58

Bertram A. and Wilma L. Huberman Book Fund for Judaica
Established by Bertram A. Huberman, '44, Wilma Leavitt Huberman, '50, HRPBA '51 and their children Danielle Alexandra, '80, Joan Robin

Mary Ann and Mose Hyman Book Fund for Judaica
Established by Jerome E. Hyman, LL.B. '47

Peter A. Isaacson Judaica Book Fund
Established by Peter A. Isaacson

Izakson-Seelenfreund Judaica Book Fund
Established by Nathan A. Low, '82

Lydia and Norman Izenstatt Judaica Book Fund
Established by Norman Izenstatt, '38

Jacker-Glazwand Book Fund for Judaica
Established by Norbert S. Jacker, '47, LL.B. '52 and Lisette Glazwand Jacker

Samuel and Fannie Jacobs Judaica Book Fund
Established by Neal A. Jacobs, '39

Dorothy and Clarence N. Jacobson Book Fund for Judaica
Established by Dorothy C. and Clarence N. Jacobson, '31

Martha and Eli Jacobson Book Fund for Judaica
Established by Phyllis J. Levine, Morey Levine, '49, Frances F. Jacobson, M. Howard Jacobson, '54, Marilyn J. Ullian, and Leonard Ullian

Jampel Judaica Book Fund
Established by Robert and Joan Jampel, Henry, '77 and Risa Jampel, Delia Jampel and John Frank, James Jampel, '85 and Sandra Marwill and Emily S. Jampel

Jastrow Family Book Fund for Judaica
Established by Peter, M.C.P. '47, Ph.D. '57 and Cornelia, B.L.A. '47 Oberlander

Judaica Library Endowment Fund
Established by alumni and friends of Harvard

Kagan Book Fund for Judaica
Established by Robert A. Kagan, '46

Benjamin Kaplan Class of 1926 and Hannah Kaplan Book Fund for Judaica
Established by Ronald F. Kaplan, '54

George M. and Dorothea L. Kaplan Judaica Book Fund
Established by Joseph P. Kaplan, '71 and Peter J. Kaplan, '76

Leonard and Janet Kaplan Book Fund for Judaica
Established by Leonard, '33, J.D. '36 and Janet, '38 Kaplan

Roger D. Kaplan Memorial Fund
Established by classmates and friends

Simon and Jennie Feder Kaplan Judaica Book Fund
Established by Mortimer Kaplan, '36

Barbara and Leo Karas Family Judaica Book Fund
Established by Barbara M. and Leo Karas, '52

Barbara M. and Leo Karas Judaica Book Fund
Established by Barbara M. and Leo Karas, '52

David and Leona Karp Book Fund for Judaica
Established by David Karp, '30

Joseph Karp Judaica Book Fund
Established by Betsy and Jack L. Karp, LL.B. '62

Simon and Frieda Kaufer Judaica Book Fund
Established by Maxwell Kaufer, '43, Jeanne A. Kaufer and their children Scott A. Kaufer, '75, Jonathan D. Kaufer and Susan M. Kaufer

Albert and Jean Kaufman Book Fund for Judaica
Established by Ann and Stephen M. Kaufman, '62

Harold J. and Golda Kaufman Judaica Book Fund
Established by Harold Jerome Kaufman, '29

Kaye Family Book Fund for Judaica
Established by Abraham I. Kaye, '19, Pearl L. Kaye, and their children Richard L. Kaye, '46, M.A. '46, Adele Kaye Cohen and David H. Kaye, '54, M.B.A. '59

Richard A. and Renee Kaye Book Fund for Judaica
Established by Richard A. Kaye, '45

Keidan Family Judaica Book Fund
Established by David B. Keidan, '66

Amanda Keidan '99 Judaica Book Fund
Established by David B. Keidan, '66

David B. and Georgia Keidan Judaica Book Fund
Established by David B. Keidan, '66

Jonathan and Amanda Keidan Judaica Book Fund
Established by David B. Keidan, '66

Isaac and Mary Kiev Judaica Book Fund
Established by Ari, '54 and Phyllis Kiev

Malcolm Kingsberg Book Fund for Judaica
Established by Harold Kingsberg, '49, M.B.A. '51

Beverly and Arthur Klein Judaica Book Fund
Established by Arthur H. Klein, '39

Philip Klein Judaica Book Fund
Established by Robert A. Klein, '48 and Caral G. Klein

Howard F. Kleinberg Book Fund for Judaica
Established by The Eugene and Estelle Ferkauf Foundation

Joshua Ari Kleinberg Book Fund for Judaica
Established by The Eugene and Estelle Ferkauf Foundation

Preston J. Kline Book Fund for Judaica
Established by Marilyn and Philip Meltzer

William I. and Martha J. Kline Book Fund for Judaica
Established by Preston J., '32 and Gertrude Kline

Ethel and Philip M. Klutznick Book Fund for Judaica
Established by Philip M. Klutznick

Matthew J. and Almena Koleman Book Fund for Judaica
Established by Matthew J. Koleman, '23

Dorothy and Theodore J. Kolish Book Fund for Judaica
Established by Melvin R. Seiden, '52

Mynue and Allan Korb Judaica Book Fund
Established by Kenneth A. Korb, '53, J.D. '56, Jaclyn P. Korb and Jason B. Korb

Korn Family Judaica Book Fund
Established by Brenda and Morton Korn, '57 and Claire A. Korn, '82

Adolph and Sally Korzenik Book Fund for Judaica
Established by Sidney S. Korzenik, '29

Frank L. and Mildred H. Kozol Judaica Book Fund
Established by Frank L. Kozol, '24, LL.B. '27

Lewis and Laura Kruger Judaica Book Fund
Established by Lewis Kruger, '56

Aaron and Lucille Landis Book Fund for Judaica
Established by Donald M. Landis, '50, LL.B. '53

Rose and Max Landsberg Judaica Book Fund
Established by Gloria and Jerry Landsberg, Steven, Jeffrey, Karen and Ruth

Adell R. Leavitt Judaica Book Fund
Established by David Leavitt, '36

Max and Celia Leavitt Book Fund for Judaica
Established by Julian J. Leavitt, '49 and Joel A. Leavitt

Michael D. and Nancy B. Leavitt Judaica Book Fund
Established by Michael D. Leavitt, '55

Louis and Rebecca Lefkowitz Book Fund for Judaica
Established by Marilyn and Stuart Troy, '59

Rabbi Daniel Isaac Leifer, Class of 1957, Memorial Book Fund for Judaica
Established by Agatha I. Leifer, Elihu I. Leifer, LL.B. '64, Myra Leifer

Dr. Jacob Lerman Judaica Book Fund
Established by his family

Sylvia and Stanley Leven Judaica Book Fund
Established by Stanley Leven, '41

Bennett H. Levenson Judaica Book Fund
Established by Leonard G. Levenson, '31

Robert and Eleanor Leventhal Book Fund for Judaica
Established by Eleanor M. Leventhal

Levin Family Judaica Book Fund
Established by Arthur L. Levin, '61, M.D. '65

Anita S. and Melvin L. Levin Judaica Book Fund
Established by Melvin L. Levin, '39, M.B.A. '41

Arthur T. Levine Book Fund for Judaica
Established by Judith Frost Levine, '51 and William Lee Frost, '47, M.P.A. '58

Barnet and Jennie Levine Judaica Book Fund
Established by Melvin C. Levine, J.D. '55

The Robert W. and Suzanne LeVine Family Book Fund for Judaica
Established by Robert W. LeVine, '59

Leonore & David Levinson Book Fund for Judaica
Established by David J. Levinson, '55, LL.B. '58

Arthur & Constance Levy Book Fund for Judaica
Established by Gregg Levy, '74, J.D. '77

Max and Irene Engel Levy Judaica Book Fund
Established by Stephen Ball Kay, '56, M.B.A. '58

Robert S. and Ceil Levy Book Fund for Judaica
Established by Robert S. Levy, LL.B. '58 and Ceil Levy, and their children Jay, Sander and Mitchell

Walter J. and Rona M. Lewit Judaica Book Fund
Established by Jane L. and Robert T. Lewit, '59, M.D. '63

Lichman Family Book Fund for Judaica
Established by J.J. Lichman, '37, M.A. '39 and Harry C. Lichman

Harold and Adele Lieberman Fund for Jewish Music
Established by the Lieberman-Okinow Families

Milton and Jeannette Lieberman Judaica Book Fund
Established by David I. Lieberman, '63, Frances S. Lieberman and Marcia H. Lieberman

Rabbi Joseph H. Lief Rabbinic Literature Fund
Established by Philip A. Lief, '37

Harry and Esther Lipson Book Fund for Judaica
Established by Charles Sidney Lipson, '54, M.D. '58 and Ellen Blotner Lipson

Littauer Hebraica Technical and Research Services Librarianship
Established by The Lucius N. Littauer Foundation

Littauer Judaica Library Student Assistantships Endowment
Established by The Lucius N. Littauer Foundation

Lucius N. Littauer Foundation Fund
Established by The Lucius N. Littauer Foundation

Nathan Littauer Fund
Established by Lucius N. Littauer, Class of 1878

Adeline Moses Loeb Book Fund for Judaica
Established by Arthur L. Loeb, '54

Joe and Emily Lowe Foundation Book Fund for Judaica
Established by The Joe and Emily Lowe Foundation, Inc.

Lowenthal-Berolzheimer-Felstiner Judaica Book Fund
Established by Alexander Lowenthal and family

Lynn R. and Jeffrey A. Lowin Judaica Book Fund
Established by Jeffrey A. Lowin, '64, LL.B. '67

Richard and Dolly Maass Book Fund for Judaica
Established by Richard Maass

Mack Judaica Book Fund
Established by Theodore Mack, '58, J.D. '61, Ellen F. Mack and their children Katherine Norma Mack, Elizabeth Ellen Mack, J.D. '88 and Alexandra Mack, '91

Anita & Michael Malina Book Fund for Judaica
Established by Michael Malina, '57, LL.B. '60

Louis David Mallet Book Fund for Judaica
Established by Dorothy M. Mallet

Mallinckrodt Book Fund for Judaica
Established by Mallinckrodt, Inc.

David E. Mann Judaica Book Fund
Established by Roberta and H. George Mann, '58

Henry Mann Judaica Book Fund
Established by H. George Mann, '58

Emanuel E. Margolies Book Fund for Judaica
Established by Michael N. Margolies, '58

Saul and Jen Shankman Margolis Judaica Book Fund
Established by Eleanor and David G. Margolis, '54

Markewich Judaica Book Fund
Established by Robert Markewich, '40, Daniel Markewich, '62, Andrew David Ball, LL.B. '65 and Eve Rachel Markewich, '83

Richard & Vivian Marson Judaica Book Fund
Established by Richard H. Marson, '55

Charlotte and Paul Massik Book Fund for Judaica
Established by Paul Massik, '38

Israel Matz Memorial Fund
Established by bequest of Sidney Matz, '21

Charles Mayer Judaica Book Fund
Established by Andrew C. Mayer, '48 and Benjamin L. Mayer, '80

Esther Melnick Book Fund for Judaica
Established by Haim H. Chiswik, '37

Herman and Adele Meltzer Book Fund for Judaica
Established by Jay J. Meltzer, '49

Etta and Norman Mendelsohn Judaica Book Fund
Established by Frederick S. Mendelsohn, '54 and Martha Mendelsohn

Laurence M. Meyer Book Fund for Judaica
Established by Ruth Meyer, Honey Meyer, James A. Meyer, '57 and Leslie H. Meyer, '67

Morris and Harriet Michelson Judaica Book Fund
Established by Morris Michelson, '24, J.D. '27

Irving and Sylvia Miller Judaica Book Fund
Established by Alfred Miller, '48, LL.B. '51

Jean Miller Judaica Book Fund
Established by Joseph M. Miller, '42

Joseph and Regina Miller Judaica Book Fund
Established by Martin and Marshall M. Miller and Families

Lawrence & Nancy Miller Judaica Book Fund
Established by Lawrence N. Miller, '49

Milstein Family Judaica Book Fund
Established by Nancy G. and Herbert E. Milstein, '58

Lena Minkoff Judaica Book Fund
Established by Harry Minkoff

Ida Davidson Mintz Judaica Fund for Exhibitions and Publications of Judaica
Established by Anna Mintz Broches and David J. Mintz, '24, M.B.A. '26

Alfred L. & Annette S. Morse Judaica Book Fund
Established by The Morse Shoe Foundation

Abraham and Rosamund Moskow Judaica Book Fund
Established by Michael B. Moskow, '55

Rose F. and Ben L. Nicholas Book Fund for Judaica
Established by Frederick M. Nicholas

Robert Arthur Novick Judaica Book Fund
Established by Bessie and Leonard Novick

Elizabeth B. and Ira L. Oppenheimer Judaica Book Fund
Established by Mr. and Mrs. Ira L. Oppenheimer, '34

Naomi and Samuel Ozer Book Fund for Judaica
Established by Mark N. Ozer, '53 and Harvey L. Ozer, '60

Jacob and Frieda Pat Endowment for Yiddish Literature and the Jewish Labor Movement in Eastern Europe
Established by Frieda Pat

Harold L. and Jane Perlman Book Fund for Judaica
Established by Harold L. Perlman, LL.B. '31

Perry Family Judaica Book Fund
Established by Ethel and Herb Perry

Charles and Elaine Petschek Book Fund for Judaica
Established by Charles I. Petschek, M.B.A. '48

Charlotte F. and Irving W. Rabb Judaica Book Fund
Established by Irving W. Rabb, '34

The Norman and Eleanor Rabb Judaica Library Student Assistantship Endowment Fund
Established by The Norman and Eleanor Rabb Charitable Foundation

Norman S. and Eleanor R. Rabb Judaica Book Fund
Established by Norman S. Rabb, '25

Isidor Rabinovitz Book Fund for Judaica
Established by Mr. and Mrs. Stuart Marks, LL.B. '44

Jacob Samuel Rayman Judaica Book Fund
Established by his father Mortimer S. Rayman, '41, his mother Ruth and his sister Eve Leah Rembrand

Samuel Rezneck Judaica Book Fund
Established by Daniel A. Rezneck, '56

David and Edra Rich Book Fund for Judaica
Established by David Rich and the Rich Foundation

Bernard A. and Edith Riemer Judaica Book Fund
Established by Bernard A. Riemer, '26, LL.B. '29

Riesman Family Book Fund for Judaica
Established by Robert A. Riesman, '40, Marcia S. Riesman and their children, Robert A. Riesman, Jr., '76 and Jean Ann Riesman, '79

David Rome Judaica Book Fund
Established by David Rome, '35, M.S. '45

Edward and Bertha C. Rose Judaica Book Fund
Established by the Bertha C. Rose Charitable Trust

Gertrude J. and Samuel Rosen Fund for Jewish Music
Established by Harris N. Rosen, '54

Lillian and Irving Rosenbloom Book Fund for Judaica
Established by Ruth and Richard S. Rosenbloom, '54, M.B.A '56

Rosenholtz Family Memorial Judaica Book Fund
Established by Mitchell J. Rosenholtz, '52

Louis E. Rosenthal Judaica Book Fund
Established by Edward Rosenthal, '56, D.M.D '60, Helen Rosenthal and their children Steven P. Rosenthal, '79, Joel H. Rosenthal, '82 and Mara Rosenthal

Marie-Louise and Samuel R. Rosenthal Book Fund for Judaica
Established by Samuel R. Rosenthal, J.D. '24

Sol Rotenberg Foundation Judaica Book Fund
Established by The Sol Rotenberg Foundation

Edmond de Rothschild Foundation Endowment for French Judaica
Established by The Edmond de Rothschild Foundation

Harold and Irma Rubenstein Judaica Book Fund
Established by Harold Rubenstein, '37, M.B.A. '40

Rubinow Book Fund for Judaica
Established by Jay E. Rubinow, '33, LL.B. '37

Max H. and Sarah R. Rubinstein Judaica Book Fund
Established by Stephan G. Rubinstein, '60

Thelma B. and Samuel R. Rudey Book Fund for Judaica
Established by Laurie G. and John M. Rudey, '65, M.B.A. '68

Rabbi Jacob Philip Rudin Judaica Book Fund
Established by Stephen I. Rudin, '53

Hilda S. Ruttenberg Judaica Book Fund
Established by Bruce R. Ruttenberg, '54

Paul Salter Judaica Book Fund
Established by Paul Salter, '21

Paul Victor Salter Family Judaica Book Fund
Established by Paul Victor Salter, '41, J.D. '44 ('48), Marjorie Kimball Salter, and their children Andrew H. Salter, '77, Sarah Salter Levy and Daniel K. Salter

Rose Sandler Book Fund for Judaica
Established by Ernest Sandler and Marvin Sandler, '54

Abraham and Anne Sapers Book Fund for Judaica
Established by Abraham E. Sapers, '21

Irving M. Saunders Judaica Book Fund
Established by Donald and Ginger Saunders

Beatrice and Harry A. Savitz Judaica Book Fund
Established by David G. Margolis, '54

Scheff Family Judaica Book Fund
Established by Hannah and Stanley Scheff, '60, Cheri Lynn (Scheff) and David Levitan, M.B.A. '88, Wendy Beth (Scheff) and Eli Wildawski, and Randi Joy Scheff

Scherman Foundation Book Fund for Judaica
Established by The Scherman Foundation, Inc.

Richard J. Scheuer Judaica Book Fund
Established by Richard J. Scheuer, '39

S. H. and Helen R. Scheuer Family Foundation Fund
Established by The S.H. and Helen R. Scheuer Family Foundation

Alice and Lewis Schimberg Book Fund for Judaica
Established by Lewis Schimberg, LL.B. '28

The Schlein Family Judaica Book Fund
Established by Herbert N., '49 and Janet B. Schlein

David R. and Shirley L. Schlossman Book Fund for Oriental Judaica
Established by Joan, Robert '59, Betty and Nancy Schlossman

Lewis M. and Josephine A. Schneider Book Fund for Judaica
Established by Lewis M. Schneider, '56, M.B.A. '60, D.B.A. '63 and Josephine A. Schneider

Schwartz Judaica Book Fund
Established by Daniel I. Schwartz, '88, A.M. '94

Leo Schwartz Book Fund for Judaica
Established by Martin D. Schwartz, '38

Harold E. Seder Judaica Book Fund
Established by Estelle H. Seder, Jonathan D. Seder, '74, Thomas E. Seder, '75 and Eric W. Seder, '79

Murray R. and Kate Seiden Book Fund for Judaica
Established by Melvin R. Seiden, '52

Dr. Rudolph L. Selig Judaica Book Fund
Established by Dorit Selig Paul, '50 and Gerald Paul

Herbert J. Seligman Memorial Fund for Judaica
Established by Lise R. Seligman

Herbert and Judith Seltzer Book Fund for Judaica
Established by Herbert A. Seltzer, '28, A.M. '29 and Judith Thurman Seltzer, '33

Daniel Ross Shapira Book Fund for Judaica
Established by The Eugene and Estelle Ferkauf Foundation

Judah J. and Florence I. Shapiro Book Fund for Judaica
Established by William Lee Frost, '47, M.P.A. '58

Melville Aaron Shapiro Class of 1926 Judaica Book Fund
Established by his daughter Jane Shapiro

Thomas Shapiro Book Fund for Jewish History and Law
Established by his children Edward Shapiro, Ph.D. '68 and Sandi Tedder

Shasha Book Fund for Judaica
Established by Alfred and James Shasha

Paul Shaw '55 Book Fund for Judaica
Established by Paul, '55, Nancy and Dory Shaw

Sher Family Judaica Book Fund
Established by Martin E. Sher, '60

Jerome N. Sherman Family Judaica Book Fund
Established by Jerome N. Sherman,'58 and Ruth Goldberger Sherman, Marc Owen Sherman, Scott Allen Sherman and Rhonda Sue Sherman

Todres Shizgal Judaica Book Fund
Established by Jerry J. Dunietz, '81

Dr. Gabriel H. Shohet Judaica Book Fund
Established by Estelle Shohet Brettman, '45

Elizabeth Klass Siegel Judaica Book Fund
Established by Joel S. Siegel, J.D. '60

Benjamin M. Sigel Book Fund for Judaica
Established by Frederica and Efrem Sigel, '64

Coleman Silbert Judaica Book Fund
Established by Lillian R. Silbert, Earl J. Silbert, '57, LL.B. '60, Josephine S. Benedek, Mimi Silbert Joseph '59, M.A.T. '63

Sisson Family Book Fund for Judaica
Established by Wallace E. Sisson, '57

Skoler Family Judaica Book Fund
Established by Laura K. and Saul Skoler, '52, M.B.A. '54 and their children, Emily V. Skoler, '82, Julie C. Skoler and Rebecca I. Skoler

Marsha & Marc A. Slotnick Judaica Book Fund
Established by Marc A. Slotnick, '64

Smith-Gill Judaica Book Fund
Established by Edward A. Smith, J.D., '42, Thomas I. Gill, LL.B. '61 and Smith, Gill, Fisher and Butts, Inc.

Alexander L.W. Snyder Judaica Book Fund
Established by Alexander L. W. Snyder, '91

Geraldine and Nathan Snyder Judaica Book Fund
Established by Nathan, '56 and Geraldine Snyder and their children Hannah and Alexander, '91

Soiefer Family Judaica Book Fund
Established by Ronald M. Soiefer, '75, J.D. '78

Hervey L. and Mildred B. Solar Judaica Book Fund
Established by Hervey L. Solar '29, LL.B. '33 and their sons Richard, '61, Barry, Robert, and Alan

Ben J. and Mary B. Solomon Judaica Book Fund
Established by Donald L. Solomon, '54 and Deidre O'Connor Solomon, M.P.H. '63

Charles L. Solov Judaica Book Fund
Established by Suzanne Solov Labiner, M.A.T. '55 and Lessing Charles Solov

Leo Sonnabend Class of 1925 Judaica Book Fund
Established by Mrs. Leo Sonnabend, Sam Sonnabend, M.B.A. '64 and Rebecca S. Leavitt

Spivak Fund
Established by William Lee Frost, '47, M.P.A. '58

Starobin Family Judaica Book Fund
Established by Oscar E. Starobin, '50, M.D. '54

Cecile Starr Memorial Judaica Book Fund
Established by William Lee Frost, '47, M.P.A. '58

Harry Starr Judaica Book Fund
Established by Harry Starr, '21, LL.B. '24

Harry Starr Memorial Book Fund for Judaica
Established by bequest of Harry Starr, '21, LL.B. '24

Jason E. Starr Judaica Book Fund
Established by Jason E. Starr, '46

Sherman H. Starr Judaica Library Publication Fund
Established by Sherman H. Starr, '46

Stein Judaica Book Fund
Established by Arthur H. Stein, '62, Barbara S. Fischer, Robert M. Stein and Edward S. Stein, '68

Alice & Joseph F. Stein Book Fund for Judaica
Established by Melvin M. Stein, '52 and Allen A. Stein, LL.B. '58

Miriam C. and Dr. Moses J. Stone Book Fund for Judaica
Established by Harris E. Stone, '56, Esta-Lee F. Stone and their children, Jordan Moses Stone and Hannah Cushing Stone

S. Robert Stone Book Fund for Judaica
Established by Marcia Stone Riesman, Robert A. Riesman, '40 and their children Robert A. Riesman, Jr., '76 and Jean Ann Riesman, '79

Julius Strauss Book Fund for German Judaica
Established by Peter Strauss, '54, M.B.A. '58

Vera and Jack Stutman Judaica Book Fund
Established by Jack Stutman, '53

Richard C. Talamo Book Fund
Established by classmates, family and friends

Caroline Tekulsky Judaica Book Fund
Established by Joseph D. Tekulsky, '44

Joseph D. Tekulsky Judaica Book Fund
Established by Patience F. Tekulsky and their children Mathew, Jo, Michael and his sister Elizabeth Tekulsky Shedlin

Max W. Titlebaum Judaica Book Fund
Established by Gerald J. Tell, '47

Benjamin A. Trustman Book Fund for Judaica
Established by Phyllis Trustman Gelfman, '56 and Robert W. Gelfman, LL.B. '56

Lester Tuchman, M.D. and George Eisenberg, M.D. Book Fund for Medical Judaica
Established by the Tuchman and Eisenberg families

Joseph and Jean Ushkow Book Fund for Judaica
Established by the Ushkow Foundation, Inc.

Harold Wald Judaica Book Fund
Established by his wife Ellen G. Wald and by his son Stephen L. Wald, '57, M.B.A. '59

Morton S. & Lillian G. Waldfogel Judaica Book Fund
Established by Morton S. Waldfogel, '44

Nathaniel and Elsie Waldman Judaica Book Fund
Established by Elsie Waldman

Waldstein Book Fund for Judaica
Established by Sheldon S. Waldstein, '45

Samuel H. Waltch Judaica Book Fund
Established by Beatrice and Jerome Spier, '49

Harry Washor, M.D. Class of 1954 Judaica Book Fund
Established by his wife Judith Washor

Cecille and Herbert Wasserman Judaica Book Fund
Established by Herbert Wasserman, '52, LL.B. '55

Judd A. and Marjorie Weinberg Book Fund for Judaica
Established by Judd A. and Marjorie Weinberg

Louis A. Weinberg Family Foundation Judaica Book Fund
Established by Stanley L. Weinberg, LL.B. '37

Rita L. Weiner Judaica Book Fund
Established by Robert S. Weiner, '44

Weinstein-Yesley Judaica Book Fund
Established by Lewis H. Weinstein, '27, LL.B. '30, Selma Y. Weinstein, '32, Sidney M. Weinstein, '39, Ethel B. Weinstein, Herschel I. Yesley, '30, M.B.A. '32, Ruth B. Yesley, Shepard H. Yesley, '35, M.B.A. '37, and Barbara C. Yesley

Harold J. and Marion Weinstock Book Fund for Judaica
Established by Harold J. Weinstock

The Weiss Family Judaica Book Fund
Established by Samuel S. Weiss, '76

Harris K. Weston Book Fund for Judaica
Established by Harris K. Weston, '40, LL.B. '43

Harris K. and Alice F. Weston Book Fund for Judaica
Established by the David F. and Sarah K. Weston Fund

Harry H. Wise Judaica Book Fund
Established by Harry H. Wise, '60, M.B.A. '66

Wishner-Loewenberg Book Fund for Judaica
Established by Elaine and Maynard Wishner and Iona and Milton Levenfeld and their friends and associates

Joseph and Hortense Wolf Judaica Book Fund
Established by Alan M. Wolf, '60 and Louise Wolf

Harry A. Wolfson Book Fund for Judaica
Established by family, friends and former students

Rudolph and Sara Wyner Judaica Book Fund
Established by Justin L. Wyner, M.B.A. '48, Genevieve G. Wyner and their children George M. Wyner, '80, Daniel M. Wyner and James H. Wyner and by The Rudolph and Sara Wyner Trust

Charles and Leah Zibbell Judaica Book Fund
Established by Charles Zibbell, '38

Harriet M. and Jerome Zimmerman Book Fund for Judaica
Established by Harriet Zimmerman, G '74

The Harry Zimmerman Judaica Book Fund
Established by Gordon Zimmerman, '52, LL.B. '55

Jacob Ziskind Book Fund for Judaica
Established by Frances Z. Goldman, Esther Z. Weltman, M.Ed. '24, Abraham Ziskind

Zurier Family Book Fund for Judaica
Established by Melvin L. Zurier, '50, Janet R. Zurier, M.Ed. '53 and their children Rebecca Zurier, '78, Benjamin A. Zurier, '83, Samuel D. Zurier and Sarah Zurier